front cover
above:
Yvonne Rainer in *Trio A*
original choreography 1966
studio photo: Jack Mitchell 1982
below:
Yvonne Rainer in front of *Privilege* poster
Hong Kong Film Festival 1991

inside front cover
street action after the invasion
of Cambodia 1970
front row: Yvonne Rainer, Douglas Dunn,
Sara Rudner

inside back cover
frame enlargement
Yvonne Rainer
Journeys from Berlin / 1971
(16mm film, 1980)

back cover
video still
*After Many a Summer Dies the Swan:
Hybrid* (videotape, 2002)
Raquel Aedo is hoisted by Rosalynde
LeBlanc, Emmanuèle Phuon,
Mikhail Baryshnikov, Emily Coates,
Michael Lomeka

This project has been supported by a grant from
the Philadelphia Exhibitions Initiative, a program
funded by the Pew Charitable Trusts, and administered
by The University of the Arts, Philadelphia.

Rosenwald-Wolf Gallery
The University of Arts, Philadelphia, PA
October 19 – November 30, 2002

Haggerty Museum of Art
Marquette University
Milwaukee, Wisconsin
September 2004 – December 2004

Other venues, until 2005 pending

ISBN–0–9627916–5–2 (paperback)
709.24–R134S

Sachs, Sid
Yvonne Rainer: Radical Juxtapositions 1961 – 2002 / Sid Sachs
Philadelphia, PA / The University of the Arts ©2003
152 p: ill., ports. c. 28cm

Catalog of an exhibition held at the Rosenwald-Wolf
Gallery, October 19 – November 30, 2002
Includes bibliographical references

Introduction – An Open Field: Yvonne Rainer as Dance
Theorist – On Being Moved: Rainer and the Aesthetics
of Empathy – Yvonne Rainer and the Recuperation
of Everyday Life – Skirting and Aging: An Aging Artist's
Memoir – E-mail Correspondence between Sabine
Folie and Peggy Phelan – After Many a Summer Dies the
Swan: Hybrid – Rainer Variations – Chronology

1. Rainer, Yvonne Exhibitions
Arts, American 20th Century
Artists United States Interviews
Artists United States Biography
1. Rainer, Yvonne
2. Rosenwald-Wolf Gallery (Philadelphia, PA)

*If any photographic credits were inadvertently omitted, correct
citations will be added in the next edition of this catalog.*

Design: Hyland/Ocko Associates

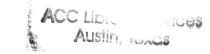

THE UNIVERSITY
OF THE ARTS®

yvonne rainer ■

■ radical juxtapositions 1961–2002

acknowledgments

The exhibition *Yvonne Rainer: Radical Juxtapositions 1961 – 2002*, the first major retrospective of the work of Yvonne Rainer, has been a complex collaborative project.

First, I want to thank Yvonne Rainer for being so generous with her world and history. Without her archives and access to her colleagues' materials, this exhibition could not have been so comprehensive. From a cold call on the telephone in the fall of 1998 to the fruition of this project in 2002, the process has been an incredible journey. This obviously could not have happened without Rainer's support and guidance. She is an incredibly intelligent, articulate person and I have been honored to work closely with her. I hope this project will inspire further investigations into Rainer's work.

This exhibition has been supported by a grant from the Philadelphia Exhibitions Initiative, a program funded by the Pew Charitable Trusts, and administered by The University of the Arts, Philadelphia. The Pew Charitable Trusts are a vital cultural asset to the Philadelphia region and the nation. I want to thank Paula Marincola and Gordon Wong of PEI for their help, grace, and patience. I was thrilled that, through this grant, Yvonne Rainer and Charles Atlas were able to create two new videos, including Rainer's first video installation in a gallery space. *After Many a Summer Dies the Swan: Hybrid* (2002) combines printed text and images to produce a heady history of art and politics in fin-de-siècle Vienna. Atlas's *Rainer Variations* (2002) turns Rainer's words and work into a montage of fact and fiction with performances—directed by Rainer—by choreographer and Martha Graham impersonator Richard Move and noted actor Kathleen Chalfant.

The dance historian Sally Banes was a guide and gracious resource to my many questions concerning choreography and performance in the early 1960s in New York. I probably would not have considered this undertaking without her previous research.

Her books have been a source of much inspiration. I miss our numerous telephone chats and e-mails. I wish her a continued recovery. Noël Carroll has been a model of professionalism both in his writing and his life during this trying time. Carroll's essay bridges the dance and cinema aspects of Rainer's career. I have truly enjoyed talking to and working with Carrie Lambert. Her work on *Trio A*'s immediacy in *October* and on the issue of empathy in Rainer's work in this catalog are models of expository excellence. The e-mail dialogue between Peggy Phelan and Sabine Folie, first published in German for the catalogue of the exhibition *Eine Barocke Party* (2001) at the Vienna Kunsthalle, was ably translated by Daniel Hendrickson. Phelan's words both here and in Rainer's *A Woman Who… Essays, Interviews, Scripts* clarify Rainer's personal and professional transitions. This personal evolution is also examined in Rainer's essay printed here.

Barbara Moore allowed me private access to hours of video interviews and an extensive Rainer exhibition at her gallery/bookstore, Bound and Unbound, in the summer of 2001. This remarkable collection of Peter Moore's photographs and Judson Dance Theater memorabilia provided my first view of many documents I had known only in print. Without the Peter Moore archives, the history of performance in New York would be less comprehensible. Mary Giese graciously granted permission for Al Giese's photographs and Warner Jepson, Robert and Evelyn McElroy, Stephanie Berger and Wendy Perron provided other resources. Zelda Wirtshafter copied *What's Happening*, her husband's film of Yam Day at George Segal's farm. Thank you to all the photographers whose work documented the ephemeral performances of the Judson Dance Theater.

Harris Fogel, the chairman of the Media Department at The University of the Arts, was responsible for getting photographic materials scanned and printed perfectly, and for providing me with the correct questions to ask Rainer. Rachelle Lee Smith of

The University of the Arts printed thirty-year-old negatives never seen before. My good friend Ed Waisnis was a great help with digital imaging expertise and video grabs while supplying requisite humor at the right moments. Nadia Hironaka did post-production video editing necessary for projection on the curved theater wall. The filmmaker Diane Pontius was vitally influential in the early stages of a preliminary Pew proposal.

Sarah MacDonald and Jadwidga Zwolska Sell of The University of the Arts' Albert M. Greenfield Library helped with needed research material. Oceana Wilson of the Crosett Library, Bennington College, Bennington, Vermont facilitated important photographic loans from the college archives. Thanks also to Matt Moore and MJ Thomas at the Fales Library of New York University for allowing me access to the Judson Memorial Church Archives and for their informative exhibition of Judson Dance Theater material in the summer of 2002. David White of Robert Rauschenberg's studio facilitated the loan of Rainer's original score for *Parts of Some Sextets* (1965) and a clear digital scan of the same. Dennis Adrian, Simon Anderson, Maurice Berger, Benjamin Buchloh, Herman Braun, John Goodyear, Debbie Haynes, Jon and Geoff Hendricks, Joseph Jacobs, Branden Joseph, Billy Linich, Lucartha Kohler, Billy Klüver, Estera Milman, Julia Robinson, Owen Smith, Sara Seagull, Jan Van der Mark, and William S. Wilson all provided vital and sometimes obscure information on various parts of the research. Thanks to John Vance at Sunship Records in Minneapolis who obtained several copies of Thurston Moore's CD *Piece for Yvonne Rainer*. Susan Glazer, Jennifer Binford, and Ninotchka Bennahum of the Dance Department and Barry Dornfeld and Craig Saper of the Communications Department of The University of the Arts have all been supportive of the project. And outside our immediate university community Ann Daly, Pat Catterson, Barry Blinderman,

Terry Fox, Bill Bissell of Dance Advance of The Pew Charitable Trusts, and Christina Sterner of the White Oak Dance Project have all been more than collegial and encouraging.

Liz Lewis was a superlative researcher and essential to the project. In addition to research, Liz had the unenviable task of organizing and scanning all notebooks and scores for reproduction. Kate Sicchio of The University of the Arts also helped with early research materials. The skills of Scott Rigby and Paul Swenbeck of the Rosenwald-Wolf Gallery staff are to be noted. They provided the knowledge to actually make the materials look right in their assigned places. I acknowledge a mystical kind of fen shui to gallery installation that only comes with experience. Bez Ocko and Sharka Hyland of Hyland/Ocko Design enabled us to present the information clearly, forcibly, and with design panache (as always). And finally I want to acknowledge, as ever, the good midwestern advice and counsel of my wife, Tara Goings, who keeps me on track whenever I waver.

Thanks to The University of the Arts for providing support and an important venue in the Rosenwald-Wolf Gallery. I hope the community in turn will thoroughly enjoy this exhibition. If I have left anyone out of these acknowledgements, it is due only to the large number of contributors to the process over the course of three years. I thank you all.

Sid Sachs, September 2002

Yvonne Rainer
in an off-off Broadway play
c. 1959

Yvonne Rainer is one of the most influential artists of the past four decades. Because at various times in her career she has been an important choreographer and also a revolutionary filmmaker, the literature on her tends to be weighted in one direction or the other. The exhibit *Yvonne Rainer: Radical Juxtapositions 1961 – 2002* and accompanying catalogue tries to correct this imbalance and approach her work from a number of critical angles.

Her work is difficult and intelligent, resisting easy categorizations. She utilizes distancing strategies and cool surfaces, disjunctive moves and layered juxtapositions that break the smooth flows of narrative and time. The work, like that of any serious artist, is ultimately about her life. She has been able to transform the facts of biography into a more universal production. The work is serious but it does not lack humor. For all her political and conceptual consciousness and her alleged minimalist coolness, there is a wry warmth and humor. Allusions to slapstick, Keystone Cops, W. C. Fields, Buster Keaton, and Carmen Miranda all pop up at various times. Her work offers its humor not as easy catharsis but as cultural reference. She uses allusion as a passage, a vehicle to further meaning.

Rainer's work locates itself in the center of various radical sensibilities of the late twentieth and early twenty-first centuries that generated The Living Theater, events, Fluxus, Minimalism, the Judson Church intermedia performances (including dance, theater, and Happenings) independent filmmaking, feminism, and the general counter-culture. In a cultural atmosphere that confuses entertainment with art, her continued commitment to avant-garde resistance is exemplary.

Rainer has written, "'Avant-garde' has always been a more meaningful term [than *post-modernism*] suggesting the continuity of adversarial cultures past and present, from fin-de-siècle Vienna to the Futurists, Surrealists, Dadaists, Fluxists, etc. Irony is indeed a

A CONCERT
OF DANCE

BILL DAVIS, JUDITH DUNN, ROBERT DUNN, RUTH EMERSON, SALLY GROSS, ALEX HAY,
DEBORAH HAY, FRED HERKO, DAVID GORDON, GRETCHEN MACLANE, JOHN HERBERT McDOWELL,
STEVE PAXTON, RUDY PEREZ, YVONNE RAINER, CHARLES ROTMIL, CAROL SCOTHORN,
ELAINE SUMMERS, JENNIFER TIPTON

JUDSON MEMORIAL CHURCH
55 WASHINGTON SQUARE SOUTH
FRIDAY, 6 JULY 1962, 8:30 P.M.

1 Yvonne Rainer, response October 6, 2001 in *The Modern /Postmodern Dialectic: American Art and Culture 1965–2000*, The Georgia O'Keeffe Museum Research Center online Symposium October 1–14, 2001, moderated by Maurice Berger.

2 Yvonne Rainer, response October 9, 2001 ibid.

key component of many of these movements, also fragmentation and rupture, ambiguity and disjuncture. I continue to identify my practice with many of these tropes, but strongly resist the conflation of irony with cynicism. Through irony we reveal social contradiction and inequity, and point to agencies of resistance. I associate cynicism with despair, with disillusionment that comes from romantic expectations. Irony is based in skepticism and struggle rather than idealism and short-term dreams of success."[1] In reference to the continuity of resistance Rainer states, "You will ask 'resistance to what?' It almost doesn't matter. Resistance to previously imposed canons of taste, to imperialism, to patriarchy, to social inequity, to war, to Abstract Expressionism, you name it. However wrongheaded, misguided, naïve, ineffectual, enraged, sublimated – a thread is there."[2]

Rainer grew up in San Francisco in an environment of radicalism. Her parents were anarchists, loosely affiliated with a group of radical Italian immigrants who settled in San Francisco before and after World War I. From her early teens she was exposed to the mix of art and politics that made San Francisco a vital cultural center. Shortly before leaving San Francisco, she was at the first reading of Allen Ginsberg's *Howl* at the Six Gallery in October 1955.

She came to dance relatively late. She studied acting with Lee Grant, but she was not successful. It seems telling that theater was her first interest and that her failure there was a failure of acting as a suspension of disbelief. She could not or would not deal with the illusionistic imperatives of traditional theater. Married briefly to the painter Al Held in 1956, Rainer associated with artists (Ronald Bladen, Nicholas Krushenick, George Sugarman) who were breaking away from the loose automatism of Abstract Expressionism into a gestural abstraction that was flatter, harder edged, and less emotionally revealing.

She studied traditional ballet, Graham technique for one year, and with Merce Cunningham for eight years. She, like others in the group that would comprise the Judson Dance Theater, came to artistic maturity through the workshops of Robert Dunn, a composer and friend of John Cage. Rainer was one of five original members of the Dunn workshop. The structure of her earliest dances was based on Cage's aleatory score for his *Fontana Mix* (1958) and she used Erik Satie's *Trois Gymnopédies* and *Trois Gnossiennes* in her *Three Satie Spoons* (1961) and *Satie for Two* (1962) respectively.[3] After that she went on to make dances that combined movements derived from observations of everyday activity and idiosyncratic imagination.

In an art world very much smaller than the present, stylistic categories were not defined as distinctly as history now records them. Rainer navigated close to the world of performance and early Fluxus as much as to dance. Fluxus, a loose movement originated by George Maciunas, dealt with the Duchampian and quotidian of the readymade in an effort to diffuse the commodification of the art market. Although later Fluxus became synonymous with comic multiples in Canal Street plastic boxes, the early events of artists such as George Brecht and Yoko Ono required only simple props and instructions that could be carried out by anyone. Ray Johnson created Nothings, and in one performance threw wooden lathes down a stair, both of which— slats and stairs—were also used by Rainer in *The Mind is a Muscle* (1966–68). In *Terrain* (1963), her dancers recited stories by Spencer Holst, a minimalist raconteur, who often read at the Judson Memorial Church and was mentioned in the *Fluxus No. 1 US Yearbook* (1962). Rainer attended performances at Yoko Ono's loft, shared a studio with Simone Forti and Forti's then husband Robert Morris, and danced *Improvisation on the Roof of a Chicken Coop* with Trisha Brown at George Segal's farm for Yam Day in 1963.[4] At the Reuben Gallery in the winter and spring of 1960–61, she saw early Happenings such as Jim Dine's *Car Crash* and performed in Forti's *See-Saw*.

3 One of Cage's enthusiasm's from the 1940s was the music of Erik Satie. Roger Shattuck's influential book *The Banquet Years* (1958) devoted a large section to Satie.

4 Yam Day was a one-day event at George Segal's farm. Part of the Yam Festival was organized by Robert Watts and George Brecht, two of the original members of Fluxus. In addition to Rainer's dance, there were activities by Wolf Vostell, Chuck Ginnever, La Monte Young, Dick Higgins's *Lecture on Dance #6* and Allan Kaprow's *Tree, A Happening*. Bud Wirtshafter's film *What's Happening* captures brief images of Rainer and Brown dancing on Segal's chicken coop roof. In Peter Moore's photograph of the same day, Wirtshafter's head and camera are visible as he films from another direction. From another vantage, Rainer watches Wolf Vostell bury a television console (see Peter Moore documentation of Wolf Vostell TV-de-coll/age action in John Alan Farmer, "Pop People," in *The New Frontier, Art and Television 1960–65* [Austin, TX, Austin Museum of Art, 2000], 53). According to William S. Wilson, Yam Day was a linguistic inversion and homage to "May" Wilson. Usually little noted is the political collectivist connotation of the inversion of May Day to Yam Day.

5   Allan Kaprow, "The Legacy of Jackson
    Pollock," *Artnews* 57, no. 6, 57.

6   Even the title of this volume recalls
    Susan Sontag's essay "Happenings:
    An Art of Radical Juxtaposition" in
    Against Interpretation and Other Essays
    (New York: Farrar Straus Giroux 1966).
    As with much appropriative art of the
    1960s, these quotations and references
    are not generated from Rainer but
    rather used by Rainer.

"Ordinariness," which in dance would become synonymous with vernacular movement, a signature of the Judson Dance Theater, was also becoming a critical issue in the visual art world. Although the Judson dancers perceived ordinariness as an antidote to the excessive drama of previous modern dance, the term can be seen as an aspect of public language (like Minimalism and Pop Art), as opposed to the heroic private codes of Abstract Expressionism. This ascendancy of the vernacular begins in the mid-1950s; there is a shift in painting in the works of Jasper Johns and Robert Rauschenberg and various assemblage artists such as Jean Follett. Allan Kaprow wrote about this tendency in an important *Artnews* essay published in 1958:

Pollock … left us at the point where we must be preoccupied with and even dazzled with space and objects of everyday life … we shall utilize the specific substances of sight, sound, *movements* (emphasis mine), people odors, touch …Young artists of today need no longer say "I am a painter" or "a poet" or a "dancer." They are simply "artists." All of life will be open to them. They will discover out of ordinary things the meaning of ordinariness. They will not try to make them extraordinary but will only state their real meaning. But out of nothing they will devise the extraordinary and then maybe nothingness as well. People will be delighted or horrified, critics will be confused or amused but these I am certain will be the alchemies of the 1960s.[5]

We all understand what running is, as we all have run, but we have not all performed a plié, which is part of the specialized language of ballet. Rainer's movement retains the populist potential that includes those who are old, non-athletic, even convalescing from surgery. Her films and choreography do not assume a grand narrative, no *Giselle*, no dying swan, no *War and Peace*. She often quotes from culture in an appropriative manner—snippets or whole texts used as objects themselves within the film and dance compositions.[6] The dances of the Judson Dance Theater took place in the same space occupied by the audience, not on a proscenium stage. In this, there are similarities

Three Seascapes
Judson Church 1963
original choreography 1962
photo: Al Giese
Crossett Library Archives, Bennington
College, Bennington, VT

film strip
MURDER and murder (16mm film, 1996)
Isa Thomas, Catherine Kellner

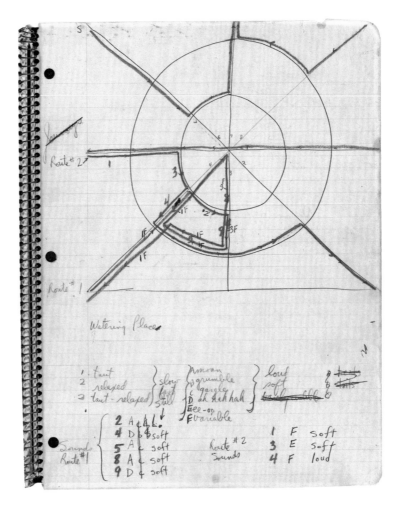

7 For example blackface by Rainer in *Untitled Partially Improvised Solo* (1964), a mask by Al Kurchin in *Garlands for Gladys* (1965), and Johns's mask of Robert Morris's face in *Site* (1964).

8 See Phelan in this catalog. A line delivered by Vladimir in Samuel Beckett's *Waiting for Godot* became the title for the Rainer-Paxton dance *Word Words*.

9 See Sally Banes, *Greenwich Village 1963: Avant-Garde Performance and the Effervescent Body* (Durham and London: Duke University Press, 1993); and Banes, *Democracy's Body: Judson Dance Theater 1962–1964* (Durham and London: Duke University Press, 1993).

with the site of some Happenings, observed from the immediate vicinity of the spectators. Being in close proximity with the dancers makes the performer more physically real (in contrast to the illusionistic personas on a stage.) Hence the dancers of the Judson Dance Theater did not play to the audience but coexisted and shared the space with them. There was no address, no eye contact, the face was a mask, a facade that did not reveal an (alleged performed, acted) inner life. Impersonality was also accomplished by use of masks and cosmetics.[7] And nudity (or partial nudity) used by Rainer in several dances such as *Word Words* (1962), *Trio A with Flags* (1970), and the Paxton stag movie prop in Rainer's *Rose Fractions* (1969) reflects counter-cultural parallels with The Living Theater, Yayoi Kusama, and Carolee Schneemann's work of the same period. The props that Rainer used were also "ordinary": a red rubber ball, a toy gun, a suitcase, steps, a lathe, a construction work barrier, a vacuum cleaner (also used by Steve Paxton in *Music for Word Words* [1963]), an eye visor, mattresses. Artists did not make these generic objects, they were not sculpturally aesthetic sets (like Noguchi's for Graham.) These objects were things with which the spectator was already familiar. They were minimal, for use in simple performative actions. Yet no matter how elementary the vocabulary, content was still in evidence. A gun, even a toy pistol, in the volatile 1960s was a loaded image. Strewn over the stage, these objects created barriers, points of location and association. The stark staging drew comparisons to Samuel Beckett's plays.[8] They also encoded specific meanings known to the audience. The red rubber ball used in *Terrain* alluded to street games. Mattresses and pillows were evocative of sleep, sex, illness, and death. Sally Banes's examination of Rainer's dance work in "Open Field: Yvonne Rainer as Dance Theorist" continues her extensive writings on the Judson Dance Theater.[9]

Rainer has often been categorized as minimalist because of her early work in dance. Her important "A Quasi Survey of Some 'Minimalist' Tendencies in the Quantitatively

Minimal Dance Activity Midst the Plethora, or an Analysis of *Trio A*" printed in Gregory Battcock's influential book; *Minimal Art, A Critical Anthology* made crucial correlations between dance and fabrication techniques in Minimalism. Although her dance shares some of operative and syntactical methods, such as the expansion of time, extended duration, and repetition, Rainer prefers the term postmodern dance to locate her choreography: "Formalism had always run neck and neck with dramatic elements in my work, which distinguished me from the Minimalists ... I never wanted to be restricted to Minimalism's anti-metaphorical strategies. In fact as a dancer I knew it was impossible: the body speaks no matter how you suppress it." [10]

Epiphanies and climaxes are finite crowd pleasers. They are what is expected of art. They cap the flow of time and create a frame for fictive resolution. Rainer's *Trio A* proceeds continually; it renounces and substitutes the traditional phrasing of dance for a continuous, immanent present. This continual present shares much with Minimalist sculpture but also relates to the extension of time in the minimalist music of her contemporaries Philip Glass and Steve Reich. [11]

Rainer's early refusal to supply easy pleasure (see her "No Manifesto") is part of a tradition of denial, a renunciation of expressionism, a refusal of narrative. Her work is anhedonic to bourgeois expectations of aesthetic pleasure and cathartic release. Rainer's dances did not provide the heroically haptic pleasures of Martha Graham or Doris Humphrey, "the exalted transformation of the performer." [12]

Rainer's film and dance, however, provide the pleasures of the text, the pleasures of the mind. For Rainer, the mind is a muscle. Her dances willfully imposed the exercise of that muscle for the viewer. Lambert's essay, "On Being Moved, Rainer and the Aesthetics of Empathy," deals with this empathetic aspect of Rainer's work in her signature dance *Trio A* and film of 1972, *Lives of Performers*.

10 Thryza Nichols Goodeve, "Rainer Talking Pictures," *Art in America,* July 1997, 58.

11 See Carrie Lambert "Moving Still: Mediating Yvonne Rainer's *Trio A*," in *October* 89, Summer 1999, 87–112.

12 See Yvonne Rainer, "Skirting and Aging" in this catalog. Also Susan Sontag wrote, "The new art and the sensibility take a rather dim view of pleasure," in "One Culture and the New Sensibility," *Against Interpretation,* 303. In 1953, Cage wrote of Rauschenberg's White Paintings: "No subject no image no taste no object no beauty no talent, no technique (no why), no idea, no intention, no art, no feeling, no black, no white (no and)," cited in Branden Joseph, "White on White," *Critical Inquiry* 27, Autumn 2000, 112.

rehearsal of *Parts of Some Sextets* 1965
photo: Al Giese
Crossett Library Archives, Bennington
College, Bennington, VT

13 Rainer quoted in Goodeve, "Rainer
Talking Pictures," 59.

In response to the Cambodian invasion during the Vietnam conflict and the censorship of Mark Morrell at the Stephen Radich Gallery, Rainer and dancers performed *Trio A with Flags* (1970) at the opening of the People's Flag Show at Judson Church, nude except for American flags. This action gave new meaning to wrapping oneself in the flag, as unpatriotic as it may have seemed to pro-war factions at the time. At Douglass College and shortly thereafter at NYU, Rainer had dancers perform *WAR*, using both real American flags and the complimentary colored (and hence distressed) version designed by Jasper Johns. After working briefly with the more improvisational collaborative group Grand Union, Rainer quit dancing in 1975.

Rainer's transition to film paralleled her transition from performer to persona. From using slides and films as props in her dances, Rainer moved to filmic narrative, at first very fragmentary, and it took over in her career. The real, the concrete, the constructed fictions of the lives of performers and actual historic events overlap in Rainer's films. Noël Carroll in his essay "Yvonne Rainer and the Recuperation of Everyday Life" further examines this line of inquiry.

Rainer's early films, such as *Lives of Performers*, are almost structuralist. Influenced by Maya Deren, Hollis Frampton, and Andy Warhol, they formally utilize live synch sound, voice-over, and inter-titles, amplifying discontinuity. But these are mere formal issues. Biographical elements, barely disguised, created a sensation to viewers in the 1970s who thought the performers were the real subjects of her films. Moreover, lines of dialogue are delivered in an uninflected manner to "invoke but not replicate the rhetoric and role-playing of disaffected love." Rainer takes up these issues in "Skirting and Aging" in this catalogue. "The stylizations of Happenings and experimental theater didn't prepare people for the kind of emotional candor and specificity they encountered in my work."[13]

Her later films took on the monumental issues of menopause, aging, housing and racism, and finally gender roles and lesbian love late in life. Narration and narrators interweave throughout the films, sometimes within the storylines, and sometimes alongside. This tradition of baroque complexity and Rainer's adaptation of masquerade is thoroughly examined in the exchange between Sabine Folie and Peggy Phelan.

Rainer's first video environment *After Many a Summer Dies the Swan: Hybrid* (2002) is also her first media project since *MURDER and murder* (1996). It montages rehearsal footage from a half-hour dance commissioned by the Baryshnikov Dance Foundation for the White Oak Project in 2000, with images of fin-de-siècle Vienna and layers them with quotations from Oskar Kokoschka, Adolf Loos, Arnold Schoenberg, and Ludwig Wittgenstein. Although the title is ironic, speaking of mortality and loss of artistic potency, it is strongly resistant, still political, and subtly humorous at points. Finally, Charles Atlas's contribution to the project, *Rainer Variations* (2002) is a wonderful video that combines documentary footage of Rainer's history and her art with its deconstruction, reconstructing and redefining history anew with surrogate performances by Kathleen Chalfant and Richard Move.

Artists often view retrospectives with trepidation. They see the process as culminative. I know what we were not able to obtain, define, and fix. I know, from first-hand contact, the degree to which her work has garnered the profound respect and admiration among her peers. I have found at least four homages to Yvonne Rainer as well as a recent museum exhibition catalyzed by Rainer's groundbreaking film *Privilege*.[14]

Yvonne Rainer: Radical Juxtapositions 1961 – 2002 is just one investigative foray, not an ultimate statement. This will not be Rainer's swan song. One thing follows another: other exhibits will follow, other essays, new films, perhaps new performances. We await Yvonne Rainer's next chapter.

14 George Brecht's *From Chapter VII of the Book of the Tumbler on Fire; for Yvonne Rainer* (1966) aka *Three of Swords,* Robert Rauschenberg's *Sleep for Yvonne Rainer* (1965), Thurston Moore's *Piece for Yvonne Rainer,* and Eleanor Antin, *Four New York Women,* object biographies shown at the Chelsea Hotel (November 1970). See Marcia Tucker and Anne Ellegood, *The Time of Our Lives* (New York: New Museum of Contemporary Art, 1999). Donald Judd named his daughter Rainer Judd after Yvonne Rainer.

an open field: yvonne rainer as dance theorist

Sally Banes

One of the most shocking aspects of avant-garde art in the 1960s was its conspicuousness of ordinary gestures, actions, rhythms, and objects. Dancers and performers combed their hair, shaved, played cards, shook hands, jogged, folded newspapers, coughed, took showers, and got dressed (and undressed); visual artists created telephones, sandwiches, ice cream bars, Brillo boxes, and soup cans; people incorporated household objects in their paintings and performances—and they called it art. To critics of the avant-garde, this radical blurring of the boundaries between art and everyday life, this arrant celebration of the banal, signaled a vulgar lack of taste and the utter disintegration of art, perhaps even its disappearance.

The choreographer/filmmaker Yvonne Rainer later recalled that in the sixties, "people said of me, 'She walks as though she's in the street!'" Her casual style was unnerving to dance audiences, Rainer explained, because at that time "if you walked as a dancer, you walked as though you were a queen, an aristocrat, a character-someone who was more than ordinary, more than human."[1]

To us, forty years later, the interest in scrutinizing the ordinary might seem like a boring proposition. But in its time this fascination with the mundane was not only shocking, it was also central to the avant-garde project of this period in all the arts. For dance it is especially crucial because the use of the ordinary was not simply an aberration or a rebellious gesture but part of a larger complex of ideas that dancers put into practice and that, articulated as a coherent conceptual framework, signaled a radical turn in dance theory. This set of ideas—about what dance is, what it should be, and what it should *not* be, as well as about why it is valuable—challenged the ways dance had been theorized in the past. This package of ideas also accounts for how postmodern dance practice could change after the 1960s while still adhering to consistent commitments and values—how an apparently Zenlike, apolitical scrutiny of dailiness could be closely related, for instance, to an anti-war dance or a feminist dance

1   *Beyond the Mainstream*, narr. Alan Titus, prod. Merrill Brockway and Carl Charlson, dir. Merrill Brockway, *Dance in America*, WNET-TV, New York, May 21, 1980.

rehearsal of *The Bells*
KQED-TV San Francisco 1962
original choreography 1961
photo: Warner Jepson

manifesto. It was a framework that linked an appreciation of ordinariness with a search for the real, and further, with suspicions about the performer's presence and notions of dance (or art) as representation, expression, and even form.

Rainer, the leading spokesperson for and practitioner of the movement, engaged radically with the historical narrative of dance theory. While Jill Johnston, the *Village Voice* dance critic during this period, wrote passionately and eloquently about the early postmodern dances from both critical and historical perspectives, it seems to me that it was Rainer who most clearly articulated a theoretical framework for postmodern dance. She constantly strove to set out in general terms what she, at least, and often other specific dancers and dances were trying to accomplish. You can see in Rainer's practice-based theory the historical progression of dance theory itself as she explores and discards one unsatisfactory traditional concept of dance after another. And while some of her own ideas may have been inspired by other artists and theorists—ranging from Bertolt Brecht to Clement Greenberg to John Cage—the way she put these notions together in both her theory and her practice created a new framework for looking at and thinking about dance. It offered a new option for dance theory.

In theorizing about her own dances and those of her peers, Rainer keeps company with other choreographer-theorists, such as Jean-Georges Noverre, Michel Fokine, and Mary Wigman. But in her theoretical predilections, she strenuously disagrees with these predecessors and with their theories of dance as imitation (in Noverre's case) and dance as expression (in Fokine's and Wigman's cases). Though Rainer and the postmoderns are sometimes called formalists and linked aesthetically with Merce Cunningham, I want to show that she also argued against this theoretical position, at least as it was formulated by the early twentieth-century critic André Levinson and the generations of his followers. To look at Rainer as a dance theorist in relation to previous dance theorists is not simply an academic exercise, for the three reigning

Three Satie Spoons
KQED-TV San Francisco 1962
original choreography 1961
photo: Warner Jepson

ideas of dance Rainer challenged—dance as imitation, expression, or (beautiful) form—remain entrenched even in the twenty-first century.

Let's look at the development of Rainer's career in relation to her practice-based theory. Born in San Francisco in 1934, the child of politically radical European immigrants, Rainer was an athletic child and an avid student. She wanted to become an actor, and she moved to New York in 1956 to pursue that career. She soon turned to dance, studying first at the Martha Graham School, then in the Bay Area with Anna Halprin, then back in New York with Merce Cunningham. In the early 1960s, Rainer danced with James Waring and improvised regularly with Simone Forti. She also read art criticism, went to gallery openings, and hung out with painters and sculptors. She, like so many artists of her generation, was deeply influenced by John Cage's ideas about breaking down boundaries between art and everyday life.[2]

In 1960 Rainer, along with Steve Paxton, Simone Forti, and others, began taking composition classes from the composer Robert Dunn at Merce Cunningham's studio. After two years, Dunn's students organized regular showings of their work at the Judson Church in Greenwich Village. The Judson Dance Theater, as this group came to be known, flourished for a short but intense period until the mid-1960s, when its members went their separate ways, many to form their own dance companies. Rainer was a leading figure of the Judson Dance Theater and presented much of her new choreography under its auspices, including the seminal *Trio A* in 1966.[3]

for language: against imitation

As early as her first piece *Three Satie Spoons* (1961), a solo that among other things incorporated vocal sounds the dancer made (both words and noises), Rainer challenged the idea that dance is a wordless art. In *Three Satie Spoons* she squeaked and

2 See Yvonne Rainer, *Work 1961–73* (Halifax: Press of the Nova Scotia College of Art and Design; New York: New York University Press, 1974), 1–10, for her autobiographical narrative.

3 On Judson Dance Theater, see Sally Banes, *Democracy's Body: Judson Dance Theater 1962–1964* (1983; reprint ed. Durham, NC: Duke University Press, 1993).

4   For full descriptions of these and other
    Rainer dances, see Rainer, *Work*, and
    Banes, *Democracy's Body*.

5   See Jean-Georges Noverre, *Letters on
    Dancing and Ballets* (1803), trans. Cyril W.
    Beaumont (1930; reprint ed. New York:
    Dance Horizons, 1975).

said, "The grass is greener when the sun is yellow"; in *The Bells* (1961), another early solo, she said "I told you everything would be alright, Harry." Her use of language in dance continued but became more complicated with such pieces as *Ordinary Dance* (1962), in which she recited a poetic, fractured autobiographical narrative, and *Dialogues* (1964), in which she and three other female dancers danced and engaged in dialogues about emotional states while three men ran on and off the stage. Later, in works such as *The Mind is a Muscle* (final version, 1968) and *Continuous Project – Altered Daily* (1970), she used long monologues and dialogues about art as "soundtracks" to her dances, thus incorporating meditations on art in a reflexive way in her own artworks.[4]

Although Rainer did not use language in every one of her dances, her practice of frequently opening up the dance performance to verbal communication of one form or another—to spoken words as well as to projected titles and extensive program notes (sometimes in the form of manifestoes)—continued throughout her career as a choreographer. On the one hand, Rainer's assertion of the dancer as a speaking subject made a proto-feminist statement about dancing women being more than mute bodies. It earned her a reputation as a thinking dancer. And on the other hand, by inserting verbal language in the dance performance, Rainer violated one of the key ground rules of dance proposed by Noverre in the eighteenth century and faithfully followed ever since: that dance is a mute art; that it has a different job to do than drama; that dance should tell its stories without resorting to speech, banners, and (Noverre sometimes said) even program notes.[5]

Yet Noverre did think that in one way dance should be like drama and thus gain status as a fine art in the emerging modern system of the arts. He thought dance should, as Aristotle explained drama did, imitate human action, tell stories. Noverre advocated what is known as the *ballet d'action*. Many theorists since the eighteenth century have disagreed with Noverre's insistence on imitation, and numerous choreo-

score for *Parts of Some Sextets* 1965
collection of Robert Rauschenberg

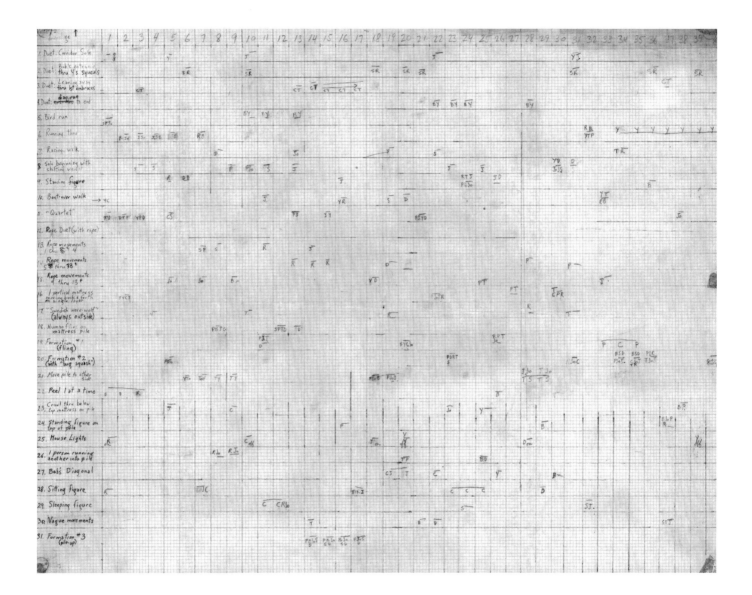

an open field: yvonne rainer as dance theorist

6   Yvonne Rainer, "Profile: Interview by
     Lyn Blumenthal," in Yvonne Rainer,
     A Woman Who: Essays, Interviews, Scripts,
     (Baltimore: The Johns Hopkin University
     Press, A PAJ Book, 1999), 61.

graphers (like George Balanchine in ballet and Merce Cunningham in modern dance) have altogether rejected the idea that dances should tell stories. Famously, Balanchine pointed out that there are no mothers-in-law in ballet. Complicated stories and relationships are the domain of novels, not dances.

Rainer's approach to narrative in her dances was complex. Rather than refusing to tell stories altogether, in works like *Terrain* (1963), she had dancers tell stories while performing unrelated movement sequences. Sometimes, she found, the storytelling and the dancing came together in unexpected ways—as when in one section, a dancer recited a story by Spencer Holst in which there was a line about his great-grandfather biting cookies into the shape of an animal and the audience connected that with the shape the dancer's body was making.[6] Rainer's use of narrative in *Terrain* was not a simple matter of denying dance's capacity to tell stories, but rather it was a critique of dance as storytelling, an exploration of the possibilities and shortcomings of dance, à la Noverre, as narration or imitation (or, in a broader sense, representation).

Writing in 1965 about *Parts of Some Sextets* (1965)—(in which an eighteenth-century minister's diary served as the "soundtrack"), while people moved mattresses, jumped on to them, handled ropes, ran, raced, crawled, and bent over—Rainer stated:

The challenge might be defined as how to move in the spaces between theatrical bloat with its burden of dramatic psychological "meaning"—and—the imagery and atmospheric effects of the non-dramatic, non-verbal theater (i.e., dancing and some "happenings")—and—theater of spectator participation and/or assault. I like to think that *Parts of Some Sextets* worked somewhere in these spaces … Its repetition of actions, its length, its relentless recitation, its inconsequential ebb and flow all combined to produce an effect of nothing happening. The dance "went nowhere," did not develop,

progressed as though on a treadmill or like a 10-ton truck stuck on a hill: it shifts gears, groans, sweats, farts, but doesn't move an inch.[7]

There are events narrated verbally, but what the dancers do are real events, what Rainer calls "movement episodes." The narration does not provide a plot or characters; the dancers are doers of work-like or sometimes dancerly actions. The incongruous friction between stories and movements or between stories and images, and the refusal, in the end, to move a story forward (even though stories may be present, they are always disrupted) are hallmarks of Rainer's work both as a choreographer and a filmmaker.

against expression

As she suggests in the passage I just quoted, Rainer was not only criticizing the narrative development or representational function of dance in her works and her writings. This passage is immediately preceded by Rainer's most famous manifesto, in which says "a very large NO to many facts in the theatre today," including "spectacle … virtuosity … magic and make-believe," and, finally, "no to moving or being moved."[8]

Some have interpreted those last six words in Rainer's statement as a denial of physical movement altogether—a call for a dance of stasis. Some years later, Rainer commented that she herself did not understand what she meant by that phrase. But clearly Rainer was discussing here not dance movement but psychological expressivity and manipulation – "no to moving or being moved" *emotionally*. Her manifesto is a refusal to participate in that particular aspect of historical modern dance; one, I might point out, that was particularly feminized. And what Rainer offered, rather than the drama of female psychological anguish, was intellectual complexity, something that had hitherto not been considered modern dance's or women artists' domain.

7 Yvonne Rainer, "Some Retrospective Notes on a Dance for 10 People and 12 Mattresses called *Parts of Some Sextets*, performed at the Wadsworth Atheneum, Hartford, Connecticut, and Judson Memorial Church, New York, in March, 1965," *Tulane Drama Review* 10:2 (T-30; Winter 1965); reprinted in Rainer, *Work*, 51.

8 Rainer, "Some Retrospective Notes," 51.

Performance
Whitney Museum of American Art 1972
Shirley Soffer, Valda Setterfield,
Epp Kotkas, James Barth
photo: Babette Mangolte

9 John Martin, *The Modern Dance* (1933; reprint ed. New York: Dance Horizons, 1965), 14.

10 Mary Wigman, "The Philosophy of the Modern Dance," *Europa*, 1:1 (May–July 1933); reprinted in Roger Copeland and Marshall Cohen, eds., *What Is Dance?: Readings in Theory and Criticism* (Oxford: Oxford University Press, 1983), 306.

The generations of choreographers before Rainer—the historical modern dancers like Mary Wigman, Martha Graham, and José Limón—thought that the body was not only universal, but that it, rather than language, was uniquely capable of revealing emotional truths. The critic and theorist of modern dance John Martin spoke of dance as the direct, unmediated manifestation (not a representation) of emotional states and identified a process similar to contagion which he called metakinesis through which dancers pass "an inexpressible residue of emotion" to spectators directly through movement.[9] Mary Wigman wrote that "the audience should allow the dance to affect it emotionally and without reserve. It should allow the rhythm, the music, the very movement of the dancer's body to stimulate the same feeling and emotional mood within itself."[10] That is, the historical modern dancers, like Graham and Wigman, believed that emotion could be crystallized and communicated directly, bypassing representation.

By the early 1960s, historical modern dance, precisely because of its emphasis on emotional expression, had become for many a pompously over-inflated, melodramatic artform. Agonies and ecstasies were the reigning emotional registers, and usually the feeling states represented—jealousy, anger, fear, and sometimes even joy—were the tortured passions of love. Rainer and others called their dance *post*-modern, and they questioned whether dissolving in an emotional flood should be the primary concern of dance (or of women choreographers). People like Rainer, Steve Paxton, and others tried to make dancing bodies into "neutral 'doer[s],'" rather than agents of affect. Perhaps influenced by Bertolt Brecht, they attempted to drain the emotional catharsis of *drama* from their performances.

Rainer was deeply influenced by the film comedian Buster Keaton, "the great stone face," in particular, his impassive visage and his close attention to performing specific tasks. For the most part, as I suggested earlier, the postmodern dancers did

not act or represent characters, but sought to *present* movement for its own sake. Rainer wrote: "The artifice of performance has been reevaluated in that action, or what one does, is more interesting and important than the exhibition of character and attitude, and that action can best be focused on through the submerging of the personality."[11] Here action does not mean imitation of action, in Noverre's sense, but presenting real activity in real time; hence the development of Rainer's (and her peers') interest in the ordinary, in tasks and daily movements that anyone can do, like walking and running.

As the sixties moved into the seventies, postmodern choreographers became more and more interested in blotting out emotion altogether. If Graham's heroines tended to dissolve in their tortured passions, in the late 1960s and early 1970s Rainer made dances that were not about love (the erotic poses and phrases in *Terrain* were deflated by the monotone voices of the dancers) but about work and the materiality and intelligence of the body.

Rainer's strategy of using non-dramatic, ordinary movement allowed her to sidestep *both* emotional expression and representation in works like *Parts of Some Sextets* (1965), in which there was recognizable dance movement but also a great deal of task-like action with ropes and mattresses. Rainer had earlier experimented with non-technical movement in other dances, like *We Shall Run* (1963), in which seven people, both dancers and non-dancers, ran in various patterns for twelve minutes to grandiose music by Berlioz. The histrionic music contrasted with the determined jog of the dancers and their calm faces to underscore the lack of an emotionally expressive dimension in the movement.

But these pieces with ordinary movement, lacking characters and psychological relationships, led her to make dances even more explicitly directed against emotional

11 Yvonne Rainer, "A Quasi Survey of Some 'Minimalist' Tendencies in the Quantitatively Minimal Dance Activity Midst the Plethora, or an Analysis of *Trio A*," in Gregory Battcock, ed., *Minimal Art: A Critical Anthology* (New York: E.P. Dutton, 1968); reprinted in Rainer, *Work*, 65.

early version of *Continuous Project –
Altered Daily*
Connecticut College 1969
Becky Arnold on the heads of David
Gordon, Douglas Dunn, Yvonne Rainer,
Barbara Dilley
photo: Ellen Levene

below:
*Untitled Partially Improvised Solo
with Bach's Toccata and Fugue
in D Minor*
Judson Memorial Church 1964
Yvonne Rainer in blackface

opposite:
Part of a Sextet
Wadsworth Atheneum 1965
original choreography 1964
Robert Morris, Yvonne Rainer
photo: Peter Moore
© Estate of P. Moore/VAGA, NYC

expression. In *New Untitled Partially Improvised Solo with Pink T-Shirt, Blue Bloomers, Red Ball, and Bach's Toccata and Fugue in D Minor* (1965) Rainer painted her face black, creating a mask that blotted out any possibility of facial affect.

Trio A (earlier known as *The Mind is a Muscle, Part 1*) and the full version of *The Mind Is a Muscle* (1966) were a compendium of Rainer's concerns, which she linked to the minimalist project in visual art. She wished, she wrote in her article "A Quasi Survey of Some 'Minimalist' Tendencies…" analyzing *Trio A*, to eliminate development, climax, and character, substituting for them equality of parts, repetition, and neutral performance. She also wished to thwart the performer's charisma, to undermine presence. She has written at length about her various strategies to achieve this aim, including the elimination of phrasing and a consistent, homogeneous use of energy, as well as averting the gaze or involving the head in movement. "The desired effect," she writes, "was a work-like rather than exhibition-like presentation."[12]

against form

Up to this point I've been discussing how Rainer disrupted narrative, representation, and emotional expression in her choreography and rejected these traditional functions for dance in her writing. But there is another aspect of her essay on *Trio A* that deserves attention; that is, her refusal of technical virtuosity, rhythm, and form. In *Trio A*, as in *Parts of Some Sextets* there was no development and barely any perceivable form. This is related to formalism, the third branch of dance theory that Rainer opposes.

Rainer writes in "A Quasi Survey" that she wants to make what she calls "movement-as-object," and states, in the program for the 1968 version of *The Mind is a Muscle*, "I love the body – its actual weight, mass, and unenhanced physicality."[13] This would seem to put her in the same formalist theoretical camp as abstract choreographers

12 Rainer, "A Quasi Survey," 67.

13 Rainer, "A Quasi Survey," 66; Yvonne Rainer, Program notes for *The Mind is a Muscle*, Anderson Theater, New York, April 11, 14, 15, 1986; reprinted in Rainer, *Work*, 71.

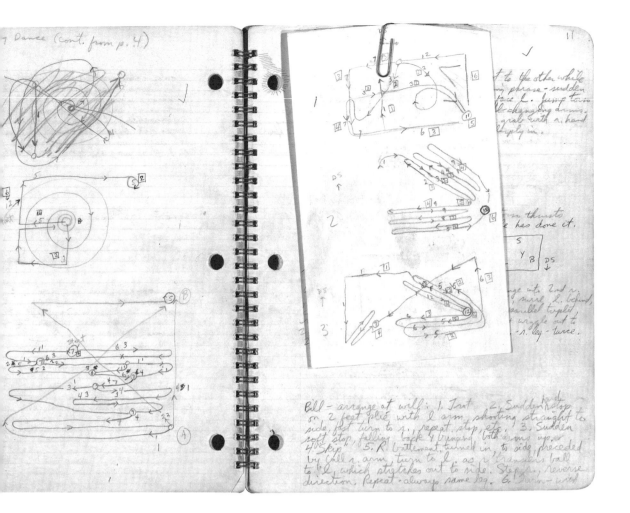

14 André Levinson, "The Idea of the Dance: From Aristotle to Mallarmé," *Theatre Arts Monthly* (August 1927); reprinted in Copeland and Cohen, *What Is Dance?*, 47–55.

like Merce Cunningham in modern dance and George Balanchine in ballet. Yet to look more closely at Rainer's theory and practice, especially in relation to dance formalism as articulated by its most eloquent and influential proponent, André Levinson, is to see that she also rejects this third option for dance. Her refusal to consider dance as form is what sets her apart from Cunningham; it is what makes his work modern and hers postmodern. Notably, Levinson's writings, celebrating the nineteenth-century Russian ballet, also set a firm foundation for Balanchine's modernism and formalism, Rainer's refusal of dance as form also sets her apart from abstract ballet.

In his famous essay "The Idea of the Dance: From Aristotle to Mallarmé," Levinson sets out a history of dance theory from the Greeks to the present; that is, 1927 when the essay was written. Levinson renders this history as a struggle between dance as story or expression and dance as movement, as abstract form. He writes: "Ever since the students of the Renaissance created the ballet … there have been two elements vying for supremacy in the dance: movement and story, abstract form and pure expression, execution and pantomime." He laments that Aristotle laid a foundation in his *Poetics* for mistaken ideas about ballet, from Noverre to Fokine in Levinson's own day. The problem with Noverre, for Levinson, is that he overlooked the intrinsic values of dancing for its own sake. It became nothing more than a wordless drama, substituting character and sentiment for its own aesthetic value. Levinson brings us back, before Aristotle, to Plato and to Socrates, who, in Paul Valéry's contemporary dialogue *The Soul and the Dance* argues *against* dance as representation. When the guest at the banquet in Valéry's dialogue, after watching a dance performance, asks what it meant, Socrates asks, "Do you not realize that the dance is the pure act of metamorphosis?" Dance's meaning, Levinson glosses, is neither expression nor imitation, but *pure function*. Thus Levinson offers a third option for dance theory, beyond imitation and expression: dance as form.[14]

opposite:
score for *We Shall Run* (1963)

We Shall Run
Wadsworth Atheneum 1965
original choreography 1963
Robert Rauschenberg, Sally Gross,
Joseph Schlichter, Tony Holder,
Deborah Hay, Yvonne Rainer, Alex Hay,
Lucinda Childs
photo: Peter Moore
© Estate of P. Moore/VAGA, NYC

an open field: yvonne rainer as dance theorist

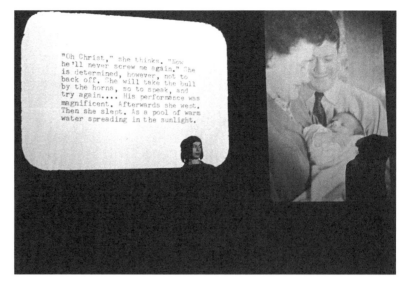

15 André Levinson, "The Spirit of the
   Classic Dance," *Theatre Arts Monthly*
   (March 1925); reprinted in Joan Acocella
   and Lynn Garafola, eds., *André Levinson
   on Dance: Writings from Paris in the Twenties*
   (Hanover, NH: Wesleyan University
   Press/University Press of New England,
   1991), 42–48.

16 Rainer, *Work*, 111.

For Levinson, this meaningfulness of dance, its pure function, is tied to an idea of beauty that inheres in the medium of dance itself. In another of his notable essays, "The Spirit of the Classic Dance," Levinson writes that he is interested in finding out what the essence of dance is. For him dancing has autonomous value, apart from representation and apart from all the other semiotic markers in the dance performance, like the costume, the music, even the libretto and its dramatic and emotional meaning. Dance is separate from the other arts, and it should be considered on its own terms, not, for instance, as a wordless drama or a moving piece of sculpture. And what are its own terms? What is its essence? For Levinson, dance is physical technique fused with beauty.[15]

I've dwelt on Levinson's ideas about dance as form partly because they remain so influential in dance criticism and theory right up to the present, and partly because they often seem deceptively close to those of Rainer and the postmodern dancers of her generation. Rainer, for instance, fulminated (in an audiotape that accompanied part of her dance *Performance Demonstration* [1968]) against even the presence of music as part of a dance: "I love dancing and am jealous of encroachment upon it by any other element," she wrote, and continued, "I want my dancing to be superstar and refuse to share the limelight with any form of collaboration or co-existence."[16] Here Rainer seems to embrace Levinson's purist medium-specificity argument—the idea that dance is (and should remain) separate from all the other arts and has its own unique essence. In 1971, during a period of purist separation of the arts that characterized the American avant-garde (as opposed to the inter-arts sensibility of both the early 1960s and the 1980s and after), Rainer wrote, again in a medium-specificity mode, about her desire to move from performance to film: "I'm no longer interested in mixed media. You either make a movie or you don't make a movie … When I recently viewed

Trio A (1966) during *Performance Demonstration #1*
Library for the Performing Arts 1968
Steve Paxton
photo: Peter Moore
© Estate of P. Moore/VAGA, NYC

several of my [short] films head-on … they seemed a boring hybrid, too obvious and simplistic to work as either film or dance."[17]

Though here Rainer expresses her desire to create a cleavage between live and recorded media (just as during the same purist period she rejected the use of music in dance), I would argue that ultimately she renounced that position, embracing medium-specificity and separatist intentions, both for her dances and for her films (for one thing, she continued to make works that had both "live" and film versions, such as *This is the story of a woman who…* (1973) and *Film About a Woman Who…* (1974), and her live performances continued to mix media). Indeed, Rainer recently commented that she departs from medium-specificity in regard to that theoretical position's search for a special essence or quality unique to dance, since walking (and running, and other ordinary movements) are actions that all people do, even when they are not dancing.[18]

Rainer's ideas about dance differ in other significant ways from Levinson's theory of dance as form. Crucially, unlike Levinson, she does not prize technique, beauty, or formal design. Thus her idea of what dance's medium might be is *not* physical technique plus beauty, but the unvarnished materiality and intelligence of the body. For her, Lenny Bruce's monologue *On Snot* belonged in a dance, as did a pregnant woman, convalescence, pain, menstruation, and fatigue, as did pleasure, power, energy, exhilaration, a black militant, and a feminist.[19]

dance as an open field

In the late 1960s and early 1970s, Rainer made several pieces, often with indeterminate structures, that collaged material from previous pieces with new material. These included *Rose Fractions* (1969), for a season of avant-garde dance on Broadway, and *Continuous Project – Altered Daily* (1970). *Continuous Project* and other works of this

17 Yvonne Rainer, unpublished essay, 1971, reprinted in *Work*, 209.

18 Yvonne Rainer, quoted in Noël Carroll, "Moving and Moving: From Minimalism to *Lives of Performers*," *Millennium Film Journal*, nos. 35 – 36 (Fall 2000), 82, fn. 5.

19 Yvonne Rainer, Program notes for *Continuous Project – Altered Daily*, Whitney Museum of American Art, March 31 – April 2, 1970; reprinted in *Work*, 131.

WAR
Loeb Student Center, New York University
1970
photo: Peter Moore
© Estate of P. Moore/VAGA, NYC

Continuous Project – Altered Daily
Whitney Museum of American Art
1970
Becky Arnold, David Gordon, Barbara
Dilley, Yvonne Rainer, Steve Paxton
photo: Peter Moore
© Estate of P. Moore/VAGA, NYC

period became multilayered in several ways. First, they were multimedia, using slides, film, live performance, music, and both written and spoken words. They were also "intermedial" in terms of performance process, since they included onstage not only finished material but also activities that were being rehearsed, learned, and taught; that is, activities that usually take place prior to the performance itself. The indeterminate aspect that emerged, especially in *Continuous Project*, of rehearsing, teaching, and learning opened a space for the performers spontaneously to discuss or even argue about what was taking place or should take place. It also allowed a space in which Rainer, the director, made visible her authorial role—as she put it, "randomly monologuing, directing, watching, disappearing, participating."[20]

20 Rainer, *Work*, 146.

This complex exploration both of the choreographer's authority and of a reflexive performance process, incorporating "backstage" behavior into "onstage" presentations, led Rainer and the dancers she worked with in new directions. One of those new directions was the performance collective *The Grand Union*, which created collaborative group improvisations from 1970–76. Another, after her long research trip to India in 1971, was to incorporate elements that had impressed her in Indian dance-drama, although she didn't directly imitate the various forms of theatre she saw there. In pieces like *Grand Union Dreams* (1971), she began dealing with mythology, characters, and fictional narratives, while still resisting and questioning imitation and representation through the use of the techniques of allusion, pastiche, parody, and self-referentiality she had already incorporated in her dances.

That Rainer incorporated so many different media and levels of performance in her performances, instilled in them the real or the ordinary, and argued for the presence of all these aspects of life and performance in dance—for an open, flexible theory of dance that contested the boundedness of artworks—in many ways makes her what I would call an "open field " theorist of dance, akin to John Cage in music, who advo-

21 Quoted in Richard Barnes, "Our
Distinguished Dropout," in Richard
Kostelanetz, ed., *John Cage*, (New York:
Praeger, 1970), 51.

22 Yvonne Rainer, "Looking Myself in the
Mouth," *October* 17 (Summer 1981);
reprinted in *A Woman Who…*, 88.

23 Rainer, *Work*, 161.

cated a blurring of the boundaries between art and life. Yet Rainer's position differs
in significant ways from Cage's. For as she has argued, Cage excluded from his field a
direct political critique. Cage, of course, was an anarchist, and that political position
informed his artistic theories and practices. Rainer acknowledges Cage's importance to
her own thinking (and to that of many artists) in regard to the inclusion of life in
art – as Cage put it, "to waking up to the very life we're living which is so excellent
once one gets one's mind and one's desires out of the way and lets it act of its own
accord."[21] Yet Rainer faults Cage for not analyzing that life in terms of its power
relations, observing that he suppresses "the question, '*Whose* life is so excellent and at
what cost to others?'" She calls, on the contrary, for making art "with a critical intelligence … not, however, so we may awaken to this excellent life; on the contrary, so we
may the more readily awaken to the ways in which we have been led to believe that
this life is so excellent, just, and right."[22]

At the height of the war in Vietnam, Rainer created several expressly political protest
works, including *WAR* (1970), which she describes as "a huge, sprawling non-competi-
tive game-like piece for 31 people … derived from terms of military tactics found
in the *Iliad*, *The Peloponnesian War*, and various accounts of the Chinese revolution and
Vietnam war."[23] The American flag served as an object in one of the rule-games in
that piece. When she was invited to participate in an artists' flag show at the Judson
Church later that year—a show organized to protest the arrests of alleged desecraters
of the American flag—Rainer created *Trio A with Flags* (1970), in which six dancers
tied flags around their necks, disrobed, and danced *Trio A* twice. She wrote that
she "felt a need for a statement with stronger political overtones" even than *WAR* had
provided, so in the *Trio A with Flags* she combined the issue of the flag with nudity.
This, she thought, created "a double-barreled attack on repression and censorship,"

and, since the purported desecraters had been war protesters, the dance functioned as an anti-war dance as well.[24]

Rainer acknowledged, years after her criticism of Cage's apolitical art, that she had been a bit harsh on him. "After all," she stated, "Cage's widespread influence occurred sometime before the art world was ready to listen to the disruptive voices of women, people of color, and lesbians and gays, all clamoring for recognition and legitimation." She went on further to propose that perhaps "Cage's notions about democratizing art helped pave the way to the airing of all those issues around race, gender, sexuality, and class that have since burst through the palace gates of high white culture."[25]

I said at the beginning of this essay that Rainer was criticized for walking "as though she's in the street!" As a theorist and practitioner, Rainer assiduously advocated dances where people could walk "like someone ordinary, someone human." While this may seem at first like a simple proposition, Rainer's work—her choreography and her theory—has probed deeply, complexly, and resonantly what it means to be a person on the dance stage.

24 Rainer, *Work*, 172.

25 Yvonne Rainer, "Commencement Address," in *A Woman Who…*, 131.

frame enlargement
Lives of Performers
Shirley Soffer, John Erdman

on being moved: rainer and the aesthetics of empathy

Carrie Lambert

Not only do I see gravity and modesty and pride ... but I feel or act them in the mind's muscles. This is, I suppose, a simple case of empathy, if we may coin that term as a rendering of Einfühlung. —Edward Bradford Titchener, 1909

This essay is based on the final chapter of my doctoral dissertation on Yvonne Rainer's performance. My thanks to Colin Beatty, Wanda Corn, Thyrza Nichols Goodeve, Janet Hess, Pam Lee, Suzanne Lewis, and especially Yvonne Rainer for comments on previous versions. David Michael Levin and Marianne Sawicki were both very generous in helping this non-philosopher develop what is a still-nascent understanding of the philosophy of empathy. Finally, I feel very lucky to have this essay published alongside writing by both Sally Banes and Noël Carroll, whose sustained critical and historical investigations of Rainer's dance and film have contributed so greatly to our understanding of it. My work depends on theirs, and I'm sure their influence will be evident throughout.

In a bare, dark room a man and a woman sit on a chair, she is perched coquettishly across his lap. They do not move. As seconds pass they breathe, but almost imperceptibly, and make only the smallest of involuntary shifts and twitches. They hold the pose. And hold it, until there is a palpable strain, both on the performers' ability to sustain the position and on the viewer's ability to pay attention to the unmoving image onscreen. Whatever the perceptual equivalent of a cramp is, we get one. And then, just when we reach the point of glancing away, the actors begin to unfold themselves. The shot cuts, opening immediately upon actors holding still another tableau.

This is a single image from the series of thirty-five *tableaux vivants* that brings to a close Yvonne Rainer's first feature-length film, *Lives of Performers* (1972). From a preceding inter-title we know the sequence is called "Final Performance/LULU in 35 shots," and viewers very familiar with the 1928 Louise Brooks classic *Pandora's Box (Lulu)* might recognize the tableaux as quotations from that film, or, more accurately as reenactments of the production stills that appear in the 1971 edition of George Pabst's film script. Needless to say, even in the context of the Pabst book the stills alone do not manage to convey the silent film's narrative (Lulu's journey from courtesan to

frame enlargement
Lives of Performers
John Erdman, Valda Setterfield, Shirley
Soffer, Fernando Torm

1 Noël Carroll, "Moving and Moving:
From Minimalism to *Lives of Performers*,"
Millennium Film Journal (2000).

2 Yvonne Rainer, "Some Retrospective
Notes on a Dance for 10 People and 12
Mattresses Called *Parts of Some Sextets*,
Performed at the Wadsworth
Athenaeum, Hartford, Connecticut, and
Judson Memorial Church, New York, in
March 1965," *Tulane Drama Review* 10:2
(T-30, Winter 1965); reprinted in Yvonne
Rainer, *Work 1961–73* (Halifax: Press
of the Nova Scotia College of Art and
Design; New York: New York
University, 1974), 51.

vaudeville star to fugitive to victim of Jack the Ripper), and when Rainer's cast reenacts the images as poses, the plot recedes still further. This in turn affects their emotional impact. Noël Carroll writes that by re-freezing still images from the melodrama, Rainer "has arrested their contagious powers." And thus the resulting poses provoke "contemplation rather than empathy, kinetic or otherwise."[1]

Certainly, the effect is nothing like the kind of emotional identification we are used to experiencing with characters on stage or screen, and of course we can not properly respond to a narrative thus fractured and stilled. And yet, I want to suggest that the viewer of Rainer's reenactments hardly sits at a cool remove from the action (or lack thereof). The twenty-second duration of each tableau is calibrated to the exact limit of both the performers' endurance and the viewer's attention. Indeed, the tension in the performers' bodies is so evident as time passes during each pose, the effort to control blinks and breaths so obvious, that it might be said that by this near-total suppression of movement, Rainer produces the most commonplace psychological effect of mainstream cinema with the least conventional means.

That is to say, we feel for them.

Empathetic experience on the part of the spectator is a founding principle of both of Rainer's chosen media—dance and film—in their conventional forms. In cinema, it is called identification; in dance, kinesthetic response. Yvonne Rainer's choreography spurned the physical and emotional heights with which dance can excite such a reaction, and her subsequent work in film deconstructed the conventions of narrative, character, and camera work that seduce us at the movies. And so we hardly think of her as an artist interested in anything so traditional as empathy. When in 1965 she famously declared "no to moving and being moved,"[2] it was surely manipulation of the viewer's physical and emotional experience that she meant to disallow. And yet, most

3 The English word comes from the
Greek *empathia*, but this antique origin
tends to obscure what the Oxford
English Dictionary as well as historians
of psychology and philosophy attest: that
there was no English word "empathy"
prior to 1909. *Empathia* is found in
Aristotle's *Rhetoric* (1441 b 32), but there
it means simply animating the inanimate.
This meaning is carried into the German
Einfühlung and the English empathy,
though both also evoke a process of *projection* that is important to me here.
On the history of empathy as word and
concept, see Gerald A. Gladstein,
"The Historical Roots of Contemporary
Empathy Research," *Journal of the History
of the Behavioral Sciences* 20 (1984); Jørgen
B. Hunsdahl, "Concerning *Einfühlung*
(Empathy): A Concept Analysis of Its
Origin and Early Development," *Journal
of the History of the Behavioral Sciences* 3
(1967); Harry Francis Mallgrave and
Eleftherios Ikonomou, "Introduction,"
in *Empathy, Form, and Space: Problems
in German Aesthetics 1873–1893* (Santa
Monica: Getty Center for the History of
Art and the Humanities, 1994), 1–85;
David Morgan, "The Enchantment
of Art: Abstraction and Empathy from
German Romanticism to Expressionism,"
Journal of the History of Ideas 57 (1996);
Lauren Wispé, *The Psychology of Sympathy*
(New York: Plenum Press, 1991).

4 Maurice Merleau-Ponty, *Phenomenology
of Perception* (New York: Routledge
& Kegan Paul, 1962). The original
French publication was in 1945
(Gallimard, Paris).

critics would agree that we miss Rainer's contribution to contemporary art if we
do not attend to the ways she experimented with her viewers' responses—physical,
imaginative, and emotional—and in this essay I want to describe a spectatorship of
"empathy, kinetic and otherwise" as central to some of her most important work.

Now, empathy is a concept with a long and intricate philosophical history, longer
and more intricate than either the casualness of the word's use in general parlance or
the recentness of its coinage would suggest (or than I could possibly do justice to
here). For despite its ubiquity in ethics, religion, therapy, and ordinary speech, the
English word "empathy" was invented in 1909, and then only in translation of a term
from German aesthetic philosophy, *Einfühlung*, literally "in-feeling."[3] In its philosophical sense, this new term denoted not compassion but a kind of projective imagining.
For the aesthetic theorists, this explained our experience of form: I project myself into
a building, a landscape, a line and feel it, as if from the inside. Then, at the beginning
of the twentieth century, the phenomenologist Edmund Husserl turned to this idea of
a projective capacity in addressing the problem of "other minds" that had troubled
Western philosophy since Descartes: how can one person ever hope to know the experience of another? Husserl proposed that we experience one another via our projective
capacity, the ability to empathize. But this was more or less a stop-gap solution. For
empathy, *in*-feeling, does not let go of the Cartesian conception of the human being as
an essentially dual creature: a mind—invisible, interior, private—and a body—visible,
exterior, public (otherwise we would not project *in*).

A number of American artists of Rainer's generation encountered one solution to
this problem in Western thought, the radical revision of the subject/object dualism
in French philosopher Maurice Merleau-Ponty's *Phenomenology of Perception*, which
circulated among critics and artists in its 1962 translation.[4] Merleau-Ponty proposed
that it is wrong to think of human beings as minds inside bodies; rather, we

5 The interpretation of Minimalism as manifesting anti-idealism as it imbricated subject and object and situated the viewer in embodied space and real time was put forward most influentially by Rosalind Krauss in the 1970s. See her "Sense and Sensibility—Reflections on Post '60s Sculpture," *Artforum* (November 1973); and *Passages in Modern Sculpture* (Cambridge: MIT Press, 1977). See also Benjamin Buchloh, "Conceptual Art 1962–1969: From the Aesthetic of Administration to the Critique of Institutions," *October* 55 (Winter 1990), especially pages 133–36. For commentary on this view, see Hal Foster's essay, "The Crux of Minimalism," in his *The Return of the Real* (Cambridge: MIT Press, 1996). It should be acknowledged that this scholarship emerges from one particular branch of the art-historical family tree. While most commentators on Minimalism share an appreciation of its peculiar relation to the viewer, not all characterize it through phenomenology.

6 This ethical aspect of the problem was also addressed by Merleau-Ponty, whose conviction of the falsity of the self/world and self/other dichotomies was a vision of an already-social human subject. Philosopher David Michael Levin explores what he sees as the implicitly socially critical aspect of Merleau-Ponty's phenomenology in "Visions of Narcissism: Intersubjectivity and the Reversals of Reflection," in Martin C. Dillon, ed., *Merleau-Ponty Vivant* (Albany: State University of New York Press, 1991).

7 Rainer, *Work*, 3. It is not difficult to see how her work in performance and especially in film (with her many ruptures of narrative time and the meta-commentaries in her inter-titles, not to mention the tendency of her characters to suddenly break into quotation of anyone from Stephen King to Michel Foucault) emerges from a distinctly Brechtian paradigm. In the category of biographical "evidence" we can also enter Rainer's cat, who goes by the name Mackie.

8 Juliet Koss, "Playing Politics with Estranged and Empathetic Audiences: Berthold Brecht and Georg Fuchs," *The South Atlantic Quarterly* 96 (Fall 1997).

pages 44–49:
frame enlargements
from *Trio A* (16mm film, 1978)
original choreography 1966

are *embodied subjects*, intertwined from the beginning with the world of things. The subject/object and mind/body dualism was a false problem. Art historians have said the Minimalist art of Rainer's contemporaries is in the legacy of Merleau-Ponty, in its staging of the perceptual encounter of subject and object, and as it answers the Cartesian view of these as distinct entities with a sense of their mutual contingency, their interconnectedness in real time and space.[5] Rainer's work of the 1960s, as we shall see, was likewise invested in an expanded and embodied form of spectatorship. But there are important differences. Rainer was a choreographer, not a visual artist, working not with plywood slabs, but with human bodies. When *she* explored the relation of subject and object, both were people.[6] This changes the stakes of spectatorship, immediately saturating the problem with ethical implications.

The stakes are even higher if we recall that Rainer's very first experience onstage was in a San Francisco theater group directed, she later recalled, by "two guys on-the-run from New York who did a lot of talking about 'epic' theater."[7] That is to say, Rainer was long familiar with the theories of Bertolt Brecht, the artist perhaps most commonly associated now with the theory of empathy, albeit with its opposite. Brecht famously argued that "theater of empathy [*Einfühlung*]," or conventional plays in which the viewer "loses herself" in emotional connection with the characters, produces passive, acquiescent spectators. To create active, critical citizens one needs to provide some kind of shock: the famous *Verfremdungseffekt*, or distanciation, of his epic theater. But Juliet Koss has recently shown that empathy remained important in Brecht's aesthetics, though he tended to suppress its continuing significance.[8] Koss argues that this is because the aesthetic theorists' idea of in-feeling had already been imported into the German theater and politicized by an ideological opponent, Georg Fuchs, who wanted to use the experience of spectatorial empathy to create "the collective right wing identity he considered necessary for a strong German state." If

the fact that she worked with bodies rather than other kinds of objects meant that Rainer, more than her contemporaries in the visual arts, immediately faced the phenomenology of perception as an interpersonal issue, it meant also that she encountered this intersubjectivity à la Brecht, as a factor of theatrical spectatorship, with the attendant psychological, and political, dangers.

To discuss Rainer's work, especially of the period 1966–72, requires a term that includes the projective activity that empathy carries from its origin in aesthetics and that points to the model of fundamental interconnection from phenomenology. But it also encompasses the simpler, and ultimately more profound connotation we are all familiar with: one person's compassionate engagement with another. Nothing else will do for a project that is, as I hope in part to show, at once so aesthetically sophisticated and so essentially heartfelt. But the *danger* of empathy, signaled by the problematic association of theatrical empathy with conventional or even politically reactionary aims, and the *trouble* with empathy, indicated in its lingering assumption of the dualistic model of personhood, are also important to keep in mind. For I believe it is precisely as a problem that fellow-feeling entered Rainer's work; a problem she set up in the choreography and analysis of her most famous dance, *Trio A*, and that she both partially resolved and deeply complicated in *Lives of Performers'* reinvention of filmic empathy.

I haven't experienced kinetic empathy in years. —Yvonne Rainer, 1970

There is a belief among some dancers, critics, and audiences that live movement performance at its best inspires a kind of experiential kinship between performer and viewer. This experience is kinesthesis, or what Clarinda Mac Low calls "body-to-body communication between performer and audience."[10] Watching a dancer move, the still viewer is meant to have an involuntary, quasi-physical experience along with him,

9 Yvonne Rainer, "Indian Journal [January 25 – February 22, 1971]," in *Work*, 180.

10 Clarinda Mac Low, "Dancing Technologies," *Dance Views*, www.danceonline.com: *Dance Online*, August 12, 1998.

11 In "Kinesthetic Communication in
Dance" (*Dance Research Journal* 16
[Fall 1984]), Mary M. Smyth subjects
the notion of kinesthetic communication
to a rigorous analysis, arguing that
it mystifies the question of what really
goes on in the perception of dance.

12 Jack Anderson, *Dance* (New York:
Newsweek Books, 1974), 9; cited in
Mary M. Smyth, "Kinesthetic
Communication in Dance," 19.

13 Judith Lynne Hanna, *The Performer –
Audience Connection: Emotion to Metaphor
in Dance and Society* (Austin: University
of Texas Press, 1983), 39.

sharing something of his body's extension, his moment of flight.[11] Kinetic response
has been proposed as the defining quality of dance itself as an art; in 1974, the critic
Jack Anderson wrote that "dance communicates because it prompts responses within
us … it appeals to our inherent sense of motion."[12] This is something very like the
early ideas of aesthetic empathy, with the difference that the object here is not a line
or a landscape or a building, but a person. As Judith Lynne Hanna defined it in 1983,
"kinesthetic sympathy occurs when we see a human body movement that we experience vicariously in our nerves and muscles; the movement evokes associations we
would have had if the original movement had been ours."[13] How does an individual
believe in and know the experience of another? Viscerally, answers kinesthetic theory.
The body has the answer to the problem of other minds.

In certain ways Rainer can be thought to have approached such a solution herself in
the dance *Trio A* (1966), when she tried to close the experiential gap between the body
of the performer and the body of the viewer. A dance with a strangely trancelike quality of movement and a kind of complex simplicity, performed at a constant, even pace
and in the mid-range of bodily extension, *Trio A* has been called a "mini-masterpiece,"
and Rainer would go on to use it in dozens of performance works over the next several decades. But none of the major innovations of its choreography—the innovations
that have made it a touchstone in the history of postmodern dance—have primarily to
do with the kind of movement of which it is made. Rather, *Trio A*'s importance
emerges from alterations to the way dance is seen. First, Rainer disarticulated the basic
building block of choreography, the dance "phrase." A conventional dance would be
made up of a number of phrases, each a complex of steps with its own beginning,
middle, and end, and a corresponding variation in degree of physical effort. *Trio A* is
a single, extended continuum of motion, in which the performer tries to suppress
any differentiation of phrases by bringing an equal level of effort to the dance's every

motion. High points are dampened, recoveries deferred. The dance becomes difficult to parse visually, like a sentencewithnospacingbetweenwords. Then, Rainer departed from dance norms by removing all repetition from this dance's choreography.[14] Conventional dances tend to be constructed of themes and variations upon them. Recurring phrases are necessary to counteract dance's inherent ephemerality: they allow the viewer a second and third view of a given sequence of movements, and create a kind of "ground" against which changes or variations can be seen. Finally, *Trio A* is remarkable for the way the choreography directs the performer's gaze. Rainer designed the movements of the head throughout the dance such that the eyes are never directed at the audience (at the one point when the dancer cannot help but face the audience head-on, she is instructed to close her eyes). While it may sound like a minor change, this aversion of the gaze has a profound effect on the spectator's experience of the dance. Thinking for a moment of the intensity with which a ballerina sparkles, smiles, and otherwise directs her energy out into the house during a solo gives some sense of how radically *Trio A* disrupts the circuit of projection, admiration, and response that Rainer in 1968 called the "narcissism, and disguised sexual exhibitionism of most dancing."[15]

The result is that *Trio A* becomes difficult to see. It can not be enjoyed by means of the psychic dynamics of desire and display, and it can't be parsed in terms of choreographic structure. This corroborates Annette Michelson's 1972 assessment that the most advanced dance of the time, including Rainer's, "pressed for an altered relationship between performer and audience, decreeing and soliciting new modes of attention and of gratification."[16] And it fits with more recent scholarship, like that of Nick Kaye, who emphasizes that the dance work of Rainer and her cohorts was characterized by "self-reflexive attention to the process of being seen."[17]

14 Save a few, transitional walking steps that show up more than once.

15 Yvonne Rainer, Program note for *The Mind is a Muscle* (1968), in *Work*, 71. The most in-depth discussion of *Trio A*'s choreography remains that of Sally Banes in her *Terpsichore in Sneakers: Post-Modern Dance* (1980; reprint ed. Middleton: Wesleyan University Press, 1987), 44 – 54.

16 Annette Michelson, "Yvonne Rainer, Part One: The Dancer and the Dance," *Artforum* 12 (January 1974), 58.

17 Nick Kaye, *Postmodernism and Performance* (New York: St. Martin's Press, 1994), 212.

"What is seen," Rainer wrote of *Trio A*, "is a control that seems geared to the *actual* time it takes the *actual* weight of the body to go through the prescribed motions ... [T]he demands made on the body's (actual) energy resources appear to be commensurate with the task—be it getting up from the floor, raising an arm, tilting the pelvis, etc.[18]"

Imagining the effect her dance will produce, Rainer proposes a spectatorship correlated with, geared to, the physical demands of dancing. As *Trio A* becomes difficult to watch *as a dance*, as the choreographic structure becomes difficult to follow and psychic gratification is deferred, "what is seen" becomes physical effort itself. In its performance what is seen will be (or will be linked to) what is felt. Rainer seems to imagine *Trio A* as a dance that bonds the apparent and the actual. It will connect the viewer's experience to the dancer's. Describing the work this way, she goes beyond mere analysis of her choreography, and produces a practiced philosophy of self and other. For if I could see what you feel, I would share your experience, experience your being.[19]

But there is a problem: the body of the performer is not one. A performing body consists of a body *felt* and a body *seen*. Or at least this seems to be what Rainer discovered with *Trio A*. For the dancer of this work exhibits a control that "*seems* geared" to the requirements of the dance; demands "*appear* to be commensurate with the task." As she makes quite clear, there is a layer of illusion involved. The performer of *Trio A* essentially creates the image of her own effort. Matter-of-factness is an effect that can be produced, just as the illusion of ease that accompanies more traditional dancing is produced. And so Rainer's *Trio A* raises the central question of kinesthetic theory: is it possible to directly correlate what the performer feels and what the audience sees? And her essay about the dance answers it in the negative; she says, "of course I have been talking about the 'look' of movements."[20] If Minimalist art is supposed to

18 Yvonne Rainer, "A Quasi Survey of Some 'Minimalist' Tendencies in the Quantitatively Minimal Dance Activity Midst the Plethora, or an Analysis of *Trio A*," in Gregory Battcock, ed., *Minimal Art: A Critical Anthology* (New York: E.P. Dutton, 1968); reprinted in Rainer, *Work*, 67. For in-depth discussion of the question of temporality in Rainer's dance, see Annette Michelson, "Yvonne Rainer, Part One," and her "Robert Morris: An Aesthetics of Transgression," in *Robert Morris* (Washington, D.C.: Corcoran Gallery of Art, 1969), 55 – 59. In the essay on Rainer, Michelson defines the "operational time" of tasklike dance in contrast to the "rhythmic, mimetic time, generated by music and/or the narrative situation of traditional dance and theatre," 58.

19 Elsewhere I have examined more closely the nature of the linkage Rainer describes between the dance as performed and the dance as seen. See my "Moving Still: Mediating Yvonne Rainer's *Trio A*," *October* 89 (Summer 1999).

20 Yvonne Rainer, "A Quasi Survey," 67.

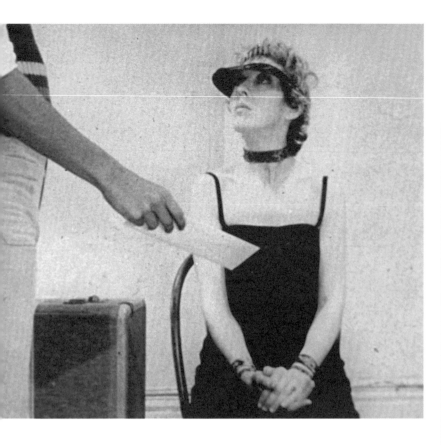

frame enlargements
Lives of Performers
Fernando Torm, Valda Setterfield

21 Rainer, 79.

22 Rainer's latest film, *MURDER and murder*, raises similar issues. Its narrative connects questions of the bodily interior and knowing the other. It simultaneously explores relationship dynamics, sexual identity, and the experience and politics of breast cancer. In a very real way the knowledge of one's *own* body reaches its limit in disease.

23 Rainer, letter to Nan Piene, January 27, 1973, in *Work*, 238.

have accomplished the anti-idealist interconnection of subject and object, in Rainer's minimalist dance their union remained a problem.

Can physical experience be shared? When Rainer found herself hospitalized at the time of a concert in which her work was going to be performed in 1967, she had her dance accompanied by a tape of her voice reading a letter written by one of her doctors regarding the severe intestinal illness she was suffering. A medical file is certainly personal, but Rainer's description of her experiment seems to exceed concerns about privacy. "I don't think I could do that today," she wrote, "at least in an instance where the biographical details belonged so exclusively to my experience, as in the case of that particular letter."[21] Now, physical suffering is the classic philosophical case for, and perhaps the most compelling life-experience of, the question of one person's ability to share the experience of another.[22] With her illness Rainer lived what *Trio A* had already taught: the limits on the communication of physicality. So much for kinesthetic empathy or the phenomenological intertwining of self and mutually constituted other; her experience of her body belonged entirely, exclusively, to her.

Rainer would reiterate this sense of the incommunicability of bodily experience, and directly address the claims of kinesthesis, just at the moment when her work turned from dance to film. In January 1973 she wrote:

Dance is ipso facto about *me* (the so-called kinesthetic response of the spectator nonwithstanding, it only rarely transcends that narcissistic-voyeuristic duality of doer and looker); whereas the area of the emotions must necessarily directly concern both of us … the more I get into it the more I see how such things as rage, terror, desire, conflict, et al., are not unique to my experience the way my body and its functioning are. I now—as a consequence—feel much more connection to my audience, and that gives me great comfort.[23]

24 The case for body or performance art as the staging of intersubjectivity, understood via Merleau-Ponty, has been made by Amelia Jones in *Body Art: Performing the Subject* (Minneapolis: University of Minnesota Press, 1998).

25 Nearly everyone who has written on Yvonne Rainer deals with the issue of her transition from dance to film. Most influential for me is an interpretation put forward by Sally Banes that deals with the difficulty modern dance history presented Rainer in terms of dealing with emotion or narrative in dance (Banes, "Yvonne Rainer's Intermediality," unpublished manuscript of a lecture given at the Women and Theatre Program conference, Toronto, Summer 1999 [n.p.]; and "Dance, Emotion, Film: The Case of Yvonne Rainer," paper presented at New York University's Humanities Center Symposium on Yvonne Rainer in April 1999). While this is an important answer to why Rainer left dance, the question remains, why film? I treat this issue in chapter 4 of my dissertation "Yvonne Rainer's Media: Performance and the Image 1961–73," doctoral diss., Stanford University, 2002.

26 This discourse is based on the combination of Althusserian Marxism and Lacanian psychoanalysis, as they converge around the idea of the positioning/ production of subjects. Of course, this literature is enormous, especially when the question is of gendered identification, and the variation of positions within it is great. However, it is important to remember that this literature almost all post-dates *Lives of Performers*, and I maintain that it is the theory of identification in its most general, even most sensible version that is most relevant to an understanding of how this particular film intervenes in conventional as well as radical modes of filmic spectatorship. Some important source essays on filmic identification are: Jean-Louis Baudry, "Ideological Effects of the Basic Cinematographic Apparatus," trans. Alan Williams, *Film Quarterly* 28 (Winter 1974–75); Christian Metz, "The Imaginary Signifier," *Screen* 16 (Summer 1975); and Anne Friedberg, "A Denial of Difference: Theories of Cinematic Identification" in E. Ann Kaplan, ed., *Psychoanalysis & Cinema* (New York: Routledge, 1990). Laura Mulvey's classic essay "Visual Pleasure and Narrative Cinema," *Screen*, 16:3 (Autumn 1975) deals with the same "territory" of the viewer's relation to the cinematic image, although not in terms of identification proper.

Also helpful is Karl Friedrich Stange, "Identification in Film Theory," Ph.D. dissertation, Northwestern University, 1984, which attends to the relevant literature preceding the rise of Lacanian film theory, like the voluntary model of identification proposed in the early 1960s by Jean Mitry. Two important books in the 1990s offered critical accounts of the Lacan/ Althusser models: Richard Allen, *Projecting Illusion: Film Spectatorship and the Impression of Reality* (Cambridge and New York: Cambridge University Press, 1995); and Judith Mayne, *Cinema and Spectatorship* (London and New York: Routledge, 1993). Rainer made her own contribution to the literature with a 1986 essay wonderfully titled: "Some Ruminations Around Cinematic Antidotes to the Oedipal Net(tles) While Playing with de Lauraedipus Mulvey, or, He May Be Off-Screen, but…" (*The Independent* 9, [April 1986]; reprinted in *A Woman Who…*), which explicates the film *The Man Who Envied Women* (1985), in which she most directly took on the issue of the gendered gaze by refusing to show the female protagonist onscreen. She asks: "Why else do we go to see narrative cinema than to be confirmed and reinforced in our most atavistic and Oedipal mind-sets?" And responds: "Well, now that I've so precipitously catapulted us into the psychoanalytic soup, I have to admit that I'm not entirely satisfied with the model of spectatorship so flippantly refashioned here" (*A Woman Who…*, 215). The theory of cinematic suture, for which the seminal texts are by Jean-Pierre Oudart ("Cinema and Suture," trans. Kari Hanet, in Nick Browne, ed., *Cahiers du Cinema 1969–1972: The Politics of Representation* [Cambridge: Harvard University Press, 1990]), and Daniel Dayan ("The Tutor-Code of Classical Cinema," in Bill Nichols ed., *Movies and Methods*, vol. 1 [Berkeley: University of California Press, 1976]) provided a related way of considering the psychic mechanism by which subjects are constructed by the devices of classic cinema, with more attention to the ways in which what Richard Allen calls "medium-awareness" are negotiated by filmic techniques. See Richard Allen, *Projecting Illusion*, 34–39. Other, non-psychoanalytic approaches to the issue of identification have been put forward precisely under the term "empathy" that I wish to remotivate here. See Dolf Zimmerman, "Empathy: Affect from Bearing Witness to the Emotions of Others," in Zillmann and Jennings Bryant, eds., *Responding to the Screen: Reception and Reaction Process*, ed. (Hillside, NJ: Lawrence Erlbaum Associates, 1991); Alex Neill, "Empathy and (Film) Fiction" in David Bordwell and Noël Carroll eds., *Post-Theory: Reconstructing Film Studies* (Madison: University of Wisconsin Press, 1996).

It strikes an odd note, especially from our current vantage at the other end of three decades of psychoanalytic film theory, to have *dance* criticized as the realm of voyeurism, and film presented as an alternative to that model of spectatorship. And it is almost a paradox that Rainer feels *less* connected to her audience in live performance, in the setting reserved in art and much art history for direct, present-tense experience.[24] But if in her most important dance Rainer had found the limit of empathy, or gone as far as she could in creating a viewer experience connected to that of the dancer, then this statement begins to make sense. As it implies, and as many commentators have pointed out, her transition from dance into filmmaking was a turn toward emotional rather than purely physical material. The issue, however, remained the same: connection.[25]

How can we say which type of film will make "people" think, or make them active, and which will not? —Yvonne Rainer, 1976

The form of connection offered by cinema is based in large part on the pleasures of identification; the experience that has over the last thirty years so neatly tied together the study of film with psychoanalytic theory.[26] For as it emerged in the 1970s, film theory deployed the concept of identification to explain that the pleasure of cinema is the result of a kind of ideological mis-recognition, à la Lacan's mirror stage, in which the film viewer involuntarily substitutes either the omniscience of the camera's view (Metz, Baudry) or the coherence and agency of the male character onscreen (Mulvey and other feminist film theorists), for her own subjectivity, by definition founded on lack or absence, and socially delimited by factors such as gender and class. In broadest outline, this process of identification both masks the subject's alienation— under modernity, capitalism, and patriarchy—and induces it. As a form of spectatorial connection, it is thus both illusory and harmful. According to film theorist Anne

27 Friedberg, "A Denial of Difference," 36.

28 For an in-depth explication and critique of the uses of Brecht in film theory, see Murray Smith, "The Logic and Legacy of Brechtianism," in *Post-Theory*.

29 Peggy Phelan makes a point of this in a recent essay on Rainer, see note 45.

Friedberg this is because "the process of identification is one of denying the difference between self and other." For "identification is a process which commands the subject to be displaced by an *other*."[27]

The model for the alternative to this kind of identification has been Bertolt Brecht's.[28] Rainer describes *Lives* as one of her more Brechtian films, and it is indeed full of distanciating techniques, some original, some Brechtian, some Brecht as filtered through New Wave cinema. Hence the characters who directly address the camera, the never-clarified narrative, the sounds of an offscreen audience's responses to the narration, a character who joins in the last third of the movie unannounced and unexplained, the avoidance of synchronized sound throughout most of the film. But it is very difficult to say that this repertoire of techniques produces any single effect on the viewer. We have seen that in practice Brecht's *Verfremdungseffekt* was meant to be alternated dialectically with techniques for producing empathy. Rainer's film is almost without conventionally absorbing cinematic techniques, but she too produced something dialectical. For the most avant-garde, alienating Brechtian techniques have a way of folding back on themselves in *Lives*, producing reinvented versions of the kind of connection they would seem to disallow.

Rainer's 1972 film predates nearly all the relevant texts in the theory of filmic identification, and so offers a fascinating view of the issue prior to the concretization of the terms in which it would be investigated in following decades.[29] If I continue to use the word empathy to describe the type of spectatorial connection produced in the film, this is not to associate Rainer's work with the uncritical theater Brecht opposed, but to motivate an alternative to the psychoanalytic model of filmic identification. Empathy, we have seen, involves projecting into, not being projected upon. In the 1909 passage that contains what may be the first published use of the word "empathy" in the English language, Titchener writes of the "mind's muscle" with which we feel

opposite:
rehearsal of *Walk, She Said*
in *Lives of Performers*
Fernando Torm, Valda Setterfield

30 See the epigraph of this essay; from the Oxford English Dictionary, 2nd edition. Edward Bradford Titchener, *Lectures on the Experimental Psychology of the Thought Process* (New York: MacMillan, 1909).

31 Banes points out that it references a specific genre, the backstage movie musical. See Banes, "Rainer's Intermediality."

32 The setting is not unlike the loft that had "starred" in Michael Snow's landmark structuralist film *Wavelength* (1967). The identity of the strange piece of furniture is not incidental. In fact, it was a pile of felt slabs left behind in Rainer's loft by Robert Morris, with whom she had lived beginning in 1964. Beyond any biographical implications (the film is known to be a kind of *roman à clef*) this provenance is significant in that the item is notably neither a proper couch nor a bed; its horizontal shape and the way it is used simply allow it to serve as a marker of "couch," or "bed." This mode of bare signification is germane to Rainer's procedure throughout the film. Transforming Morris's slabs into home furnishing, and in particular into such emotionally loaded items as couch and bed, also corresponds with what Rainer has called "the emotional underbelly of Minimalism" (text accompanying Rainer's installation, *Inner Appearances*, Vienna Kunsthalle, 2001).

33 Annette Michelson summed up the effect of the New York milieu succinctly in 1974 (before, of course, going on to more in-depth analyses): "*Lives of Performers* is, among other things, the construction of a series of rather joyless *marivaudages*, in which protocols and autoanalytic exchanges are invested with the high-minded austerity of Sohoesque life." Annette Michelson, "Yvonne Rainer, Part Two: Lives of Performers," *Artforum* 13 (February 1974).

34 Actually, there are two men, Fernando and John, but they sometimes seem to be the same character; in any case it is the relationships of two women to a single man that gives the film its thematic center.

35 Where color marks the difference between Kansas and Oz, in Rainer's film the difference between real time/place and remembered incidents is clearly marked by the character Valda, who wears rolled-up overalls to rehearse, but who stands out among the dungareed performers in a floor-length evening gown in all the scenes bracketed by the rehearsals.

emotions or sensations we observe in others.[30] If in *Trio A*, also called *The Mind is a Muscle, Part 1*—Rainer found the limits of how this muscle could be stimulated in the viewer of live performance, in *Lives of Performers* she extended it. As she moved from dance to film, empathy was moved from the physical to the social.

Lives of Performers is a 90-minute, black-and-white film. Feature-length and concerned, as its title indicates, with the behind-the-scenes lives of a group of dancers, it has always been considered to point toward cinematic convention in subject matter while remaining firmly located in the experimental rather than mainstream film canon.[31] Though Rainer flirts with narrative in the rendering of a backstage love triangle, the paratactic, deadpan, and otherwise avant-gardist qualities of her performance work are very much in evidence in a film whose *mise-en-scene* might be described as classic pre-Soho: an expansive, wood-floored loft, slightly shabby, nearly bare, sparsely furnished with mismatched chairs and a bed or couch covered with a thin, patterned spread.[32] Peopled by youngish, white men and women in bellbottoms, harem pants, and sweater-coats, *Lives of Performers* presents the very picture of an avant-garde New York milieu circa 1970. The lighting, for the most part, is even and flat; the costumes nearly all pedestrian. Occasional reflexive shots of a script, camera, or Klieg light within the film further certify its avant-garde pedigree.[33]

At the broadest level, *Lives* is a sort of group flashback during which members of a performance troupe discuss their interrelationships, centering on a love triangle between a man and two women.[34] It opens and closes (save the final "Lulu" tableaux) with scenes of the group rehearsing a dance in the loft. In gross outline, then, the structure resembles Hollywood classics like the *Wizard of Oz*, beginning and ending with scenes of a time and place we recognize as "real," while the bulk of the film takes place somewhere, or, as in this case, sometime else.[35] We transition into this "reminiscence" (the narrative time of the film is by no means clear or simple) not with the

on being moved: rainer and the aesthetics of empathy

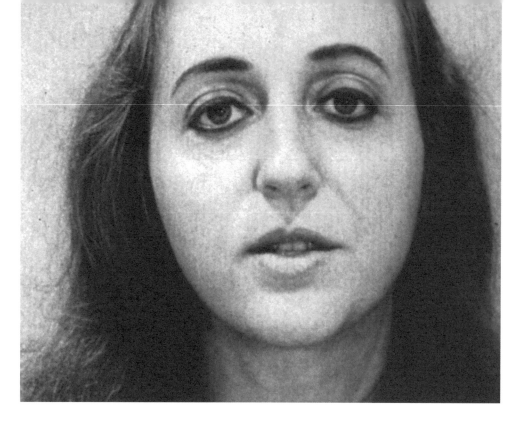

frame enlargement
Lives of Performers
Shirley Soffer: "Which woman is the
director most sympathetic to?"

36 This reprises the situation Rainer had
produced four years earlier in *Act*,
which was a section of her performance
piece *The Mind is a Muscle* when a group
of dancers arranged themselves slowly
into a series of abstract tableaux, while
across the stage a magician performed
juggling and magic tricks.

37 As many have pointed out, it is not for
nothing that Rainer subtitled *Lives of
Performers* "A Melodrama." Peggy Phelan
and B. Ruby Rich, among others, have
drawn important connections between
the film and the feminist discussions of
Hollywood melodrama that appeared
in the years following it. I want to add to
this that it is not only the subject matter
and form but also the kind of attention
we pay to films about relations and
emotions that is at issue in *Lives*; the
shorthand for this mode of viewing
being "identification."

tinkling music or slow fade of conventional flashbacks but with a series of long
close-ups on photographs strewn atop a pile of typewritten papers—shots just
as punishing of filmic expectations and audience endurance as the final *Lulu* "stills."

These images document a performance of Rainer's dance *Grand Union Dreams* in
a New York gymnasium in May 1971. Because photographer Susan Horowitz documented the piece primarily with long shots across the gym, the photographs consist
of wide stretches of light wall and pale floor, with the dancers relatively small, dark
shapes on the gray expanse. As we try to find areas of interest in one after another of
these still images filling the frame, we hear a voiceover in which Rainer, Shirley Soffer,
Valda Setterfield, and Fernando Torm talk about what happened during rehearsals
and performances (of the pictured dance, we assume): what they each felt; what they
remember thinking of one another; when it was that certain feelings developed;
which conversations they recall.

Pale, distant images and almost gossipy discussion of personal lives, gray, homogenous
stills and tantalizing narration: this sequence calls for two radically different attentive
paradigms, one befitting difficulty-seeking denizens of the avant-garde, the other more
seductively entertaining.[36] Perhaps the sugar helps the medicine go down, but on the
other hand, the dry, documentary images can also be conscience-saving palliatives,
giving avant-gardists in the audience permission to indulge a taste for melodrama. In
this way, the juxtaposition of attentive modes serves as a sort of overture for the
dialectics of the film to come.[37]

Listen, for example, to the way the characters' conversation during the progression of
dance stills comprises a series of misunderstandings or, rather, mismatched versions
of certain moments. "I wondered why you didn't touch me," says Valda. Fernando
replies: "I stood on the landing beside the doorway as we were going back downstairs.

38 Valda on messages Fernando left for her: "That really confused me—not that I thought much about it in a personal way—but rather, you know, in that way you do when you are trying to figure out someone else's intentions, whether or not they are directed at you." That activity of "figuring out someone else's intentions" is basic to the film—and of course basic also to the interpretive endeavor. This and all further quotes from the film are taken from the *Lives of Performers* film script published in Yvonne Rainer, *The Films of Yvonne Rainer* (Bloomington: Indiana University Press, 1989), 59–76. A version of the script was also published in Rainer's *Work*, but not all speeches are given in full in the earlier publication.

39 While in dance eye contact with the audience creates the emotional connection most dancers cultivate, in the fiction-dependent worlds of theater and film, the situation is reversed. Talking to the camera is a classic way to cut into the manipulative identification that films create, and with it Rainer might be said to be refusing the filmic equivalent of kinetic response. Laura Mulvey's seminal essay, first published three years after *Lives of Performers'* release, saw the "conscious aim" of narrative film to be as "always to eliminate intrusive camera presence and prevent a distancing awareness in the audience. Without these two absences (the material existence of the recording process, the critical reading of the spectator), fictional drama cannot achieve reality, obviousness, and truth." And in the essay's final paragraph, calling for a radical cinema, she announces that "the first blow against the monolithic accumulation of traditional film conventions (already undertaken by radical film-makers) is to free the look of the camera into its materiality in time and space and the look of the audience into dialectics and passionate detachment" (Mulvey, "Visual Pleasure," 25–26).

I thought you'd have to squeeze through." At which Valda groans: "O God! You gave me so much room." The missed moment of intimacy mirrors other instances of communication gone wrong—"we started to argue, only it wasn't an argument because I simply repeated my opinion while you repeated yours," remembers Shirley. In effect, in the voiceover the characters are reconstructing the period during which their relations complicated, while outlining the miscommunications out of which their intimacy nevertheless emerged.

Likewise we curious and confused viewers, who have been given no introduction and few clues about the characters or their situation—who don't even see the people who are speaking—are busily reconstructing as well, attempting to connect the characters' statements in some kind of narrative sense. For us, too, it is out of disruptions in the mode of communication that intimacy paradoxically evolves. And so, while inhibiting the pleasure of narrative in this scene by jumbling the story, and disallowing "visual pleasure and narrative cinema" by filling the screen with still photographs instead of sound-synched moving images of the characters, and even while emphasizing with stories of mismatched perceptions the difficulty in achieving fellow-feeling or connection, Rainer nonetheless creates a kind of empathetic link between spectator and speaker in this scene, viewer and character. For on each side of the screen, so to speak, people try to make sense of the emotional developments the soundtrack describes.[38]

Something similar happens during the film's most classically Brechtian moment. The characters have been discussing a film they have seen in which the plot centers on a love triangle between a man and two women. At the end of the conversation, Shirley looks straight into the camera and asks "which woman is the director most sympathetic to?" This direct address ruptures the conventions of cinema, and would normally be considered a tactic to prevent the audience from slipping into the filmic fiction.[39]

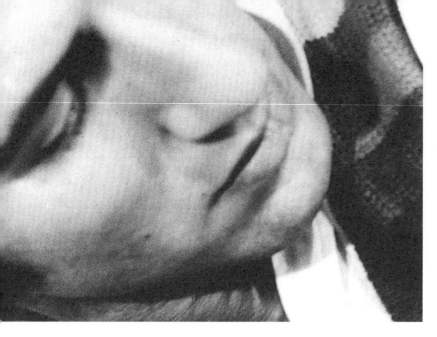

frame enlargement
Lives of Performers
Fernando Torm
Yvonne Rainer voice-over: "See, there's
a lot of time..."

opposite:
rehearsal of *Walk She Said*
in *Lives of Performers*

But it works differently here. Shirley asks which woman the director is more sympathetic to, but that is to say, to which of the two women (simultaneously the women in a film discussed by the characters and the characters themselves) the director (at once of the discussed film and the one we are watching) is most sympathetic. Because of the conflations so carefully arranged between the movie being watched and the movie being discussed *in* the movie being watched, the direct address technique becomes less alienating than, well, *friendly*. If the fictional protagonists we watch are sitting around talking about a movie, does being asked a question about the film keep us outside emotional identification, or invite us into the conversation?

It is telling that Shirley's direct address is a rare moment of synchronized sound in *Lives of Performers*. But just as her question both brings us out of the film and into the conversation, the mismatch of image and sound in the rest of the film has an ambiguous effect. After the transition from the "present" time of the dance rehearsal via the sequence of still photographs, the bulk of the film consists of shots of actors conversing in various configurations in the bare loft. While we watch these images, we hear the characters discuss themselves in the third person: "Shirley is saying how she put it off as long as she could," says Shirley, as we see an image of Shirley moving her lips. Though this voice-over is not synchronized (we do not see the character speak the words we hear) it *is* cued to the image (we hear words correlating with the images we see, filling us in on background information or describing the thoughts of a character whose actions we are watching). We soon realize that the speaking Shirley, Yvonne, Fernando, and then Valda are, or were, watching a projection of the film's image-track at the time they recorded its sound. Rainer confirms this by commenting to the other actors as the image pans around the loft and over the images of their bodies—"See, there's a lot of time … you don't have to talk all the time, just put in an occasional comment … I mean, you don't have to fill up that time with everything that may be

going on"—an instruction that instantly makes it clear that their task has been to discuss what is going on in the real time of the projected film. Likewise, Fernando at one point reads a line, "But the only answer he gets is, 'Do you have any money?'" only to be interrupted, first by Yvonne—"That comes a little later ... There!"—and then Shirley—"She says, 'Do you have any money?'" All of this is much to the recorded audience's amusement as the image "catches up" to Fernando's mistake.

Theodor Adorno suggested, and Jonathan Crary has more fully argued, that the reign of capitalism's culture industry was secured in the late 1920s, the time of the first talkie, for it was synchronized film sound that finally produced the fully absorbed and passive mode of spectatorship on which the future of commercial culture depended.[40] Rainer's de-synching disrupts just this mode of comfortable absorption as it continually removes us from the events on screen. Thus it follows Brecht's dictum very closely: "taking the incidents portrayed and alienating them from the spectator."[41] But, despite the disruption of talkie convention, it must be noted that there is also an evident effort in *Lives* to maintain a *correspondence* between the film's images and voices. The voices must hurry up, or pause, to keep their narration cued to the images. This is synchronization of a different kind, with very different effects. It draws attention to the limits on the spectator's perception of another's interior life, as the characters describe feelings and thoughts that we could not have gathered even from sound-synchronized images experienced in "real time." But here is another of the doubled-back, hairpin turns in spectatorship that characterizes *Lives*, for the new synchronization *defines the actors as viewers of the film*, viewers not unlike ourselves.

The bulk of *Lives* is narrated by people watching it, specifically, watching images of themselves within it. The effect of this exercise manifests itself first in Shirley's delighted voiceover reaction to her first close-up: "I look like an old-time movie star!" It is at once clear that the speaking Shirley is watching the filmed Shirley, that the

40 See Jonathan Crary, "Spectacle, Attention, Counter-Memory," *October* 50 (Fall 1989).

41 Bertholt Brecht, "Short Description of a New Technique of Acting Which Produces an Alienation Effect," in John Willett, ed. and trans., *Brecht on Theatre: The Development of an Aesthetic* (New York: Hill and Wang, 1964), 136.

frame enlargement
Lives of Performers (1972)
Shirley Soffer, Valda Setterfield,
Fernando Torm, John Erdman
"In *Lives* everyone sees."

opposite:
production still of *Valda's Solo*
Lives of Performers
original choreography 1971
photo: Babette Mangolte

42 Erving Goffman's *The Presentation of Self in Everyday Life* (Garden City, NY: Doubleday, 1959) is a classic study of social interactions as performance. Rainer herself suggested the relevance of this book to her work, although admittedly in a conversation in which I had introduced the topic of the media-influenced condition of everyday life. Interview with the author, June 1999.

character is split in time and made a viewer of herself. This is the mis-recognition fundamental to the psychoanalytic accounts of film spectatorship. Like the baby before the mirror, Shirley enjoys the falsely coherent (or in this case, falsely glamorous) image of herself.

If in the classic cinematic setup the viewer identifies with the male figure who has the power of the gaze, in *Lives* everyone sees. But everyone only sees. All the characters are onlookers, and so are we. We are bound together by our spectatorship and under its conditions. Lives of performers are lives of spectators. Not only is social life a performance, à la Erving Goffman, but if we are always performing, then we are also always watching the performances of others, and of ourselves.[42] In Rainer's film, we are involved with the characters not in spite of but because of their disconnection from their own images. We recognize rather than mis-recognize; we make a connection *in alienation rather than in empowerment*.

One of the strange effects of the mode of narration-by-viewer is that we see what conversation looks like without hearing it, while we hear things we cannot see. Toward the end of the film John and Shirley have a discussion about a recent performance of hers. Or rather, Yvonne reports on their discussion, while we watch the two characters silently converse:

"Shirley is asking John what he thinks of the performance, what he thought of the last performance. And he liked some of it, and some of it he disliked intensely. He was in such a bad mood at the end of it that he couldn't even applaud and he couldn't come backstage. He apologizes; he says, 'You wouldn't want me to pretend I was enthusiastic when I wasn't, would you?' And she says, 'No … but I'm sorry that you can't take pleasure in a friend's success' [audience laughter]."

43 There may have been some personal feelings involved in the audience's response as well, for Rainer has often indicated that aspects of the relationships in *Lives of Performers* were taken from her own very recent past.

44 Buchloh, "Conceptual Art 1962 – 1969"; Foster, "What's So Neo About the Neo-Avant-Garde?"; Foster, "The Crux of Minimalism."

45 Peggy Phelan is most incisive on this point, for she is at pains to remind viewers that Rainer's films emerge from the concerns of her dance work and not from feminist film theory (which they in many cases predate). See Phelan, "Yvonne Rainer: From Dance to Film." I find this an exemplary rejoinder to those accounts of Rainer's work that seem to work backwards, finding the theory of the gendered gaze in dance works like *Trio A*, and rendering them feminist statements. While understandable, and certainly suggestive, this interpretive move detracts from the particularity of what *Trio A* (performed just as often by men as women) accomplished *vis à vis* the relation of performer and spectator, which was both necessary for and larger than a gender critique. See Mark Franko, "Some Notes on Yvonne Rainer, Modernism, Politics, Emotion, Performance, and the Aftermath," in Jane C. Desmond, ed., *Meaning in Motion: New Cultural Studies of Dance* (Durham, NC: Duke University Press, 1997). In her return to performance with *Trio A Pressured* (1999), Rainer seems to have wanted to get at the issue of the gaze. A new duet version of *Trio A* has a male performer accompany Rainer as she dances, hovering over, walking around, and diving under her as he follows an assigned task: to keep her face in his line of sight at all times (no easy feat given the choreography that keeps the head away from the audience and in constant motion). Characteristically, this maneuver complicated rather than clarified any relationship between *Trio A* and theories of the gaze.

I love this passage, partly for the way Shirley cuts to the vanity and jealousy that are such a large and unspoken part of the history of art, but even more for the way it alters the terms in which Rainer approaches the question of spectatorship, of viewer and viewed.[43]

It is by now a truism in art history that while turning attention to the viewer of art rather than (or in addition) to the object, Minimalist art assumed an essentially asocial viewer, neutral in terms of gender, race, and class.[44] Rainer's investigations of spectatorship in her dance work of the same period are often no more specific, but several critics have also pointed out that through her interest in the dynamics of viewing, which she describes early on as a matter of voyeurism and narcissism, sexually charged, even her early works raise the terms that would become so central to feminist film theory with the publication of Laura Mulvey's "Visual Pleasure and Narrative Cinema" in 1975.[45] With the little episode of John's self-interested response to Shirley's performance, spectatorship is rendered not only perceptual but social.

An even more poignant and telling instance of this newer approach to spectatorship serves as a kind of dénouement for the film. Valda tells Fernando (actually, Fernando's voice tells us that Valda tells him) that she wants to show him something. An inter-title flashes: "Valda shows Fernando her solo." When it is removed we are in a sleeker, cleaner space than the loft, though also unfurnished and bare-walled. In this elegant new space (actually the Whitney Museum of American Art) Valda performs a slow-paced solo. For a Rainer dance, the solo is oddly elegant. Rainer wrote that Valda's "movements are executed in silence, vaguely resembling those of a temptress in a silent movie, and lit by an encircling follow-spot." She has indicated that the movement was inspired by the Nazimova performance in the silent movie *Salome*.[46] However, the elegant drama of the dance is cut somewhat by the fact that even as she maintains a haughty, temptress-behooving demeanor, Valda is manipulating a child's

rubber ball, which she rolls down her arms, draws across her body, and holds, just as elegantly as possible, beneath her chin.

The rubber ball appeared once earlier in the film, bounced by a little girl, as Shirley, in voice-over, recounted a dream about pure, free physical activity. The ball-bouncing scene is the baby version of Valda's solo; the solo the grown-up form of the dream. In this ball-borne connection across the film, the dream of the kind of dance Rainer had earlier espoused—a dance that would not be self-conscious, that would convey physicality alone—is undone. "Valda *shows* Fernando her dance"; the museum setting further emphasizes the idea of display; and the follow-spot literally highlights questions of viewership. Modified by the focusing attention of eye, camera, and projector, it seems that dance, for Rainer, has taken on rather than overcome the inevitable distinction between doing and viewing. Dance is not capable of conveying the feeling of the moving body; we are left with the body seen. At the beginning of the film Valda voiced the performer's side of what Rainer called "that narcissistic-voyeuristic duality of doer and looker," when she said about Fernando's romantic attention to her that "it was like the excitement of performance, experiencing my beauty and value when all those eyes are focused on me." When she shows him this solo, his attention and the attention of performance are conjoined and coupled, of course, with the gaze of the spectator.

John disliked Shirley's performance, and when Valda shows hers to Fernando, his response is less than enthusiastic as well. His voice explains:

Fernando is saying to her why did she show him that, that he has seen it a hundred times. Then she says that she does it differently now, that she understands it better. But he says that it looks the same to him.

46 Rich, "Yvonne Rainer," 6.

47 Quoted in Koss, "Playing Politics."

She does it differently now; to him it looks the same. With this, we are back with *Trio A*'s question of the internal and external knowledge of a dance; what she feels does not correspond to what he sees. But in the context of the relationships traced in the film, this non-correspondence is socially, emotionally inflected. Or perhaps a better word is *infected*, for Fernando's dismissal of the performance she has offered him seems mean-spirited. Either annoyed or insensitive, he has *decided not to see*. In the context of avant-garde practices, this idea—that attention is determined by sex, desire, and anger, affected by jealousy and pride—fundamentally changes the rules of the game. For it transforms what it means to be an active viewer. Always assumed to be the desideratum of the avant-garde, here, suddenly, we are reminded that in fact we are always active insofar as we cannot see without also extrapolating to our own situations, making assumptions, or bringing prejudices to bear. It takes effort to produce spectatorial empathy and it takes effort to refuse to.

Read a work on gorki [sic] and me—ideology, ideology, ideology ... the whole thing is like a description of a dish in which nothing is said about the taste.[47]
—Bertolt Brecht

There is something delicious about Rainer's production of empathy in the Lulu stills at the end of *Lives*, extracting extravagantly emotional images from a melodrama, submitting them to a multi-level process of mediation (film to still to book to pose and back to film), and then extending the analyzed, flattened ghosts of the original images to a breaking point at which the viewer has an empathetic reaction despite it all. In doing this, she takes the intended response to the original 1928 film—emotional identification—and rather than negating it, transforms it, correlating, if not connecting, the performers' experience to our own. Her device invites acknowledgement of our connection to another in his or her embodiment, in a way that reflects the insights

of phenomenology, while also inserting layers of misfit and mediation that remind us always of the differences between bodies seen and felt.[48] Later in her career, Rainer laconically cribbed the conventional wisdom on avant-garde spectatorship as "disjunction equals alert viewer equals critique of patriarchy and narrative coherence equals passive viewer equals status quo."[49] The tiredness she imputes to this formula was already apparent when she eschewed its rigidity in favor of her first film's hairpin turns of engagement. *Lives* allows the spectator connection while disallowing union.

There is pleasure in this narrative cinema, and it is the supposedly retrograde pleasure of identifying and even kinesthetically bonding with characters. But it comes only if we ourselves pay attention and are willing to projectively imagine; that is, if we become alert viewers after all. In Rainer's version of empathy, it seems, we move ourselves.

48 The aspect of Rainer's accomplishment I want to stress here resembles the notion of empathy as extrapolated by the philosopher Edith Stein, a student of Husserl, who in her 1916 *On the Problem of Empathy*, strove for a definition of the term that, unlike the earlier uses of the concept in aesthetics, would not imply "oneness": "The subject of the empathized experience, however, is not the subject empathizing, but another … while I am living in the other's joy, I do not feel primordial joy. It does not issue live from my 'I.' Neither does it have the character of once having lived like remembered joy. But still much less is it merely fantasized without actual life." Edith Stein, *On the Problem of Empathy*, trans. Waltraut Stein (Washington, D.C.: ICS Publications, 1989), 11 – 12.

49 Noël Carroll, "Interview with a Woman Who," *Millennium Film Journal* 7, 8, 9 (Fall 1980 – Winter 1981); reprinted in *A Woman Who…*, 178 .

production still
Film About a Woman Who...
(16mm film, 1974)
Dempster Leach, Renfreu Neff
photo: Babette Mangolte

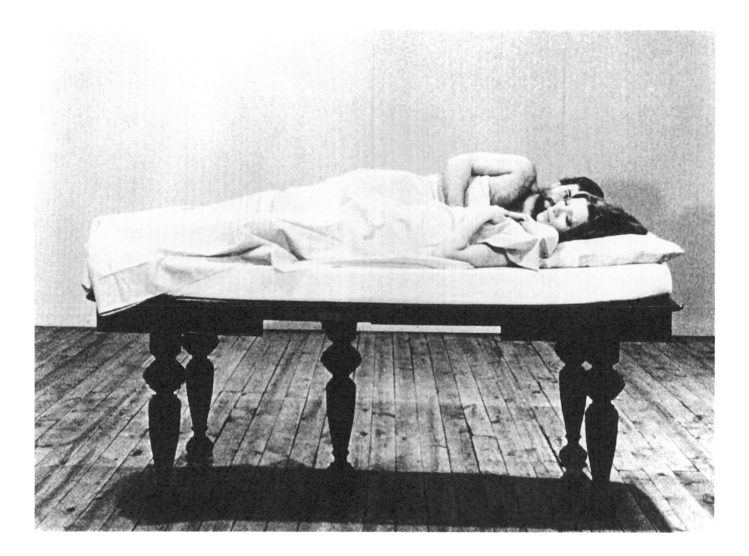

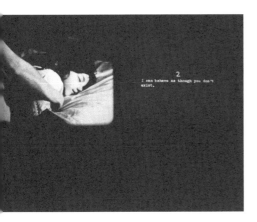

film and slide projections
This is the story of a woman who...
Theater for the New City 1973
Sarah Soffer
photo: Babette Mangolte

yvonne rainer and the recuperation of everyday life

Noël Carroll

f or over four decades, Yvonne Rainer has commanded attention as a leading American artist. She first attained notoriety as a dancer and choreographer in the early 1960s as a pioneer of the Judson Dance movement, but then, in the 1970s, she launched a second career as a major avant-garde filmmaker, starting with her first feature-length film *Lives of Performers* (1972). When performance art was emerging as a distinctive artform in the 1970s, Rainer also contributed to the medium, staging her early films before shooting them. As well, she is a writer, not only of the scripts of her films but of occasional pieces, including manifestoes and autobiographical sketches, or most often, mixtures of these two modes in highly allusive, juxtapositional pastiches.[1] Needless to say, summarizing the achievement of an artist of such varied endeavors is impossible. Instead, in this essay, I will try to provide something of an overview of her career by tracing one (I stress *one*) of her abiding themes as a way of introducing her work to a broader audience.

One constant across Rainer's oeuvre is her commitment to avant-garde forms of address. Her choreography challenged audiences to place it—a pressing task, since it was shorn of the orienting frameworks that generally accompany dance like narrative, expressivity, repetitive choreographic schemas and decorative ornamentation. Viewers were put in a situation where they had to question what they were seeing as well as why they were being shown it.

In her films, performance pieces, and writing, we are also confronted with disjunctive structures, fragmentary narratives, allusions, quotations from other authors (literary, theoretical, and cinematic), all juxtaposed in a way that taxes the audience to make sense of them. Rainer is an artist who affords little space for what is sometimes called "passive spectatorship." Through strategies of defamiliarization[2] and juxtaposition, she calls upon audiences to reflect on and to find significance in her work, not merely in the sense of reconstructing its meaning but more importantly in terms of reflecting on

1 For example, see Yvonne Rainer, *Work, 1961 – 73* (Halifax: Press of the Nova Scotia College of Art and Design; New York: New York University Press, 1974); Yvonne Rainer, *The Films of Yvonne Rainer* (Bloomington: Indiana University Press, 1989); and Yvonne Rainer, *A Woman Who… Essays, Interviews, Scripts* (Baltimore: The Johns Hopkins University Press, 1999). The latter two books also include extensive bibliographies of Rainer's writings.

2 On the importance of defamiliarization as a strategy in the art-making of the 1960s, see Sally Banes, "Gulliver's Hamburger," in *Everything Was Possible: Dance in the Sixties*, Sally Banes, ed. (Madison, WI: University of Wisconsin Press, forthcoming).

frame enlargement
Journeys From Berlin/1971
(16mm film, 1980)
Cynthia Beatt

what that meaning implies about the world outside the work and our commerce with that world.

If Rainer's means, including defamiliarization and radical juxtaposition, are formidably avant-garde, what are the subjects she uses these means to interrogate? There are, of course, many. But one subject that recurs throughout her work is the everyday, and this theme can provide a through-line that may connect her varied experiments across the arts. In her choreography and dance, this concern with the everyday manifested itself in a preoccupation with ordinary movement—walking, running and performing everyday tasks. Historically, theatrical dance movement was extraordinary, virtuoso, dramatically and expressively charged, and/or decoratively complex. In contrast, Rainer, was interested in restoring an appreciation of what was wondrous in simple, everyday movement and in leveling the distance in social esteem between, say, a jeté and mattress moving.

Turning to film, Rainer expanded her palette to encompass the lives as well as the movements of her performers. But these were the everyday lives of her performers, their romantic intrigues and betrayals as they occur without what Rainer regards as the supercharged supplements of Hollywood sentimentality—glamorous close-ups, romantic music, strained coincidences, lavish sets, *Good Housekeeping* color coordination, and the like.

Engaging everyday sexual relations in *Lives of Performers, Film about a Woman Who…* (1974), and *Kristina Talking Pictures* (1976) brought Rainer in contact, in the early 1970s, with a robust, emerging feminist movement. Though never subscribing uncritically to the various sorts of feminist theories that were abroad at the time, Rainer's encounter with feminism and other forms of progressive political thinking in the seventies did encourage her to adopt a perspective on everyday life that had been promoted in

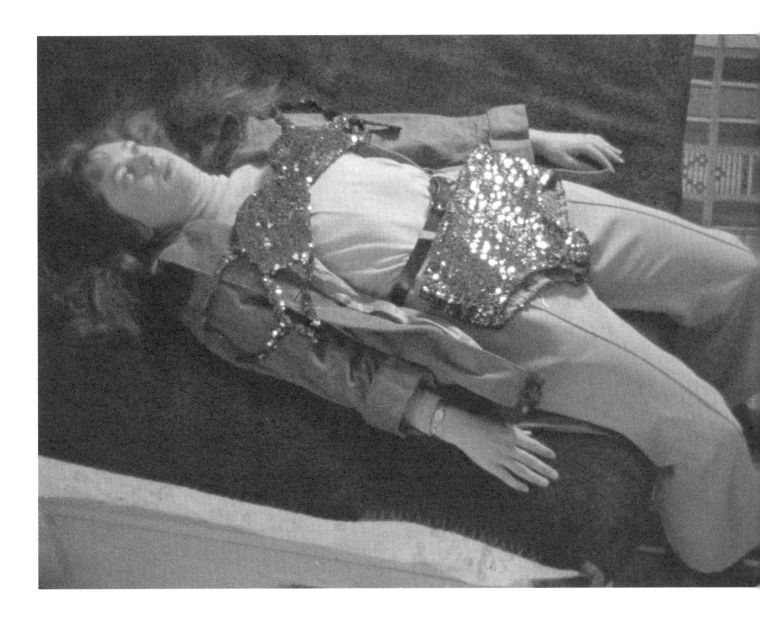

yvonne rainer and the recuperation of everyday life

The most remarkable thing was
the silence that emanated from
friends and family regarding
the details of my single
middleage. When I was younger,
my sex life had been the object
of all kinds of questioning,
from prurient curiosity to
solicitous concern. Now that I
did not appear to be looking for
a man, the state of my desires
seemed of no interest to anyone.

various ways by much radical thinking throughout the twentieth century: viz., the everyday is a site of significant political struggle. With respect to feminism, the so-called battle of the sexes was not merely an artifact of human nature, but rather was implicated in larger social issues and part of a larger movement of human emancipation.

Though Rainer was influenced by this critique of everyday life, she did not accept wholeheartedly various simplifying mantras of the late 1970s and the early 1980s, such as "the personal is political." She granted that these realms could be connected, and parts of her films illustrate this vividly. However, she was also cognizant that the personal and the political could come apart in ways that defied issuing summary judgments about agents and their actions. In *Journeys from Berlin/1971* (1980) and then in *The Man Who Envied Women* (1985), Rainer explored the disconnect between the personal and the political, questioning whether personal rage always originates in justifiable political outrage, suggesting that the latter may sometimes function as a mask for the former, and indicating how political rectitude can also be a counter in the politics of seduction.

Rainer's interrogation of the notion that the "personal is political" informs her perspective on the everyday in her subsequent films, *Privilege* (1990) and *MURDER and murder* (1996). In both, the personal and the political, everyday life and larger social struggles coexist and often even intersect. But for Rainer, neither term in the equation reduces without remainder to the other.

In *Privilege*, Rainer brings to the fore the topic of menopause—a feature of everyday life, an eventual experience for every woman—but one rarely subject to public acknowledgment in film or art. In *MURDER and murder*, she makes lesbian domestic life and its tensions—another occluded fact of the everyday life of our culture—her focus, along with exploring the pressure that a mastectomy can bring to such a

frame enlargement
The Man Who Envied Women
(16mm film, 1985)
William Raymond

opposite:
frame enlargement
Privilege (16mm film, 1990)

relationship, and, for that matter, to a heterosexual relationship. And though Rainer uses the film as a platform to voice many of her suspicions of the medical-pharmaceutical complex, the film is not simply an accusation of political-economic machinations; it is also the story of the mutual adjustment of two minds (and bodies) in love.

Though the personal and the political frequently converge and the latter often shapes or at least has impact on the former, Rainer observes there is also life to be negotiated outside of politics as well. And it is this complexity of the interrelationships and nonrelationships between the personal and the political in everyday lived existence that has become one of the enduring marks of Rainer's project as a filmmaker.

In Rainer's films, these dimensions of everyday life and others rub against each other, sometimes (even often) intruding on each others' space, but also sometimes passing each other by. Rainer is interested in both the connects and the disconnects in this often disconsonant array. Though her style is avant-garde, in her attention to the everyday, to the convergences and divergences of the forces that mold it, to its contradictions, its structures, its incongruities, and untotalized messiness, she is some kind of realist. Certainly, her subject matter is realist inasmuch as she is preoccupied with the everyday, albeit not the everyday life of the working class, but, more often than not, the everyday existence of artists and intellectuals. Nevertheless, perhaps there is also a way in which her highly disjunctive style of presentation contributes to her variety of realism too. For all those disconnects in her exposition would appear to do something to recuperate the non-narrativized, jostling, often unclosured tempo of everyday life.

Death Solo during *Terrain*
Judson Memorial Church 1963
Yvonne Rainer, Albert Reid, William Davis
photo: Al Giese
Crossett Library Archives, Bennington
College, Bennington, VT

Solo Section during Terrain
Judson Memorial Church 1963
William Davis, Yvonne Rainer,
Steve Paxton
Photo: Al Giese
Crossett Library Archives, Bennington
College, Bennington, VT

below:
Satisfyin' Lover
choreography by Steve Paxton
St. Peter's Church 1968
Photo: Peter Moore
© Estate of P. Moore/VAGA, NYC

rainer's choreography and ordinary movement

Rainer first came to public notice in the early sixties as a member of the Judson
Church dance movement, which is often cited as the fountainhead of what is called
postmodern dance.[3] Other members of the group included Steve Paxton, Trisha
Brown, David Gordon, Deborah Hay, Lucinda Childs, and Judith Dunn. A recurring
theme in the work of the choreographers and dancers of the Judson group was
ordinary movement. In one composition, for example, Steve Paxton ate a sandwich,
while in his dance *Satisfyin' Lover*, a crowd of people, including a substantial number of
non-dancers, walked across the stage, dressed in everyday attire, ambling just as they
might walk down the street.

Rainer, as well, experimented with ordinary movement. In *We Shall Run* (1963), she
enlisted non-dancers wearing street clothes and set them jogging for seven minutes.
In *Terrain* (1963), the choreography includes such ordinary movements as flicking one's
hair, opening mouths, scratching ears, touching toes, creeping, stretching, lying as
if sleeping, and sitting up. Performers, when not actively engaged in the dance, stood
behind barricades, as one might while watching a parade, though, at one point, they
move the barricade, like a piece of furniture. The theme of moving heavy objects also
reappears in *Room Service* (1963) and *Parts of Some Sextets* (1965), where in both pieces
the performers move mattresses.

In *Trio A* (1966), Rainer's signature dance, the movement is not precisely everyday
movement; it is not what you would expect to see in a mall. It is complex and
possesses what Kant would call "purposiveness without a purpose." But the energy
expenditure required, as opposed to that required by ballet or modern dance, is closer
to that of ordinary action and movement. *Trio A* could be, and often was, performed
by non-dancers. What Rainer was after here and elsewhere was "a more-matter-of-fact,

3 For an account of postmodern dance,
see Sally Banes, *Terpsichore in Sneakers:
Post-Modern Dance* (Boston: Houghton
Mifflin Company, 1980). For a history of
the Judson Church dance movement,
see Sally Banes, *Democracy's Body: Judson
Dance Theater 1962–1964* (Durham, NC:
Duke University Press, 1993).

4 Rainer, *Work*, 65.

5 For comments on the difficulty of
   construing Judson-type dances as move-
   ment-as-such, see Noël Carroll and
   Sally Banes, "Working and Dancing," in
   Aesthetics: A Critical Anthology, George
   Dickie, Richard Sclafani, and Ronald
   Roblin, eds. (New York: St. Martin's
   Press, 1989).

more concrete, more banal quality of physical being in performance"[4] than was to be found in the reigning, virtuoso dance traditions of the time. In order to achieve this quality, she modeled her choreography on ordinary movement, that demanded no particular, specialized, trained, dancerly skill.

One way of explaining the quest for the quotidian in the choreography of Rainer and her peers is to correlate it with parallel developments in the fine arts, notably Minimalism. Minimalism, among other things, was committed to stripping art down to its basic elements, exploring shapes as a physicist might study atoms. It was a reflexive search for the "building blocks" of art. The Minimalist painter wanted to disclose what painting really was: to reveal that the real subject matter of art was not the "illusionistic" (in the rhetorical language of the day) dramas of saints and pagan gods found in Renaissance frescoes, but rather shape and space.

Similarly, some of the Judson choreographers, including Rainer, were interested in establishing the quiddity of dance—dance as it really was, shorn of the dramatics of a Martha Graham and the spectacles of American Ballet Theater. And in their reductionist fervor, the Judson choreographers settled on movement, as such ordinary acting and doing as the essence of dance. When Judson dancers walked or jogged across the stage, they were not intended to be portraying walking or jogging; they were, it was believed, walking and jogging (while, perhaps ironically, and not altogether consistently, also signaling their conviction that dance is just movement as such).[5] This was a kind of "realism" that motivated modernists in the fine arts to move from the ocular realism of perceptual verisimilitude to ready-mades as following a sort of inexorable logic.

However, though the association of Rainer with the aims of Minimalism tells part of the story, her commitment to exploring everyday movement, I think, has other sources

Swarm during *Rose Fractions*
Billy Rose Theater 1969
photo: Peter Moore
© Estate of P. Moore/VAGA, NYC

as well. For Rainer seems to me to belong to a tradition that reaches from William Wordsworth through Ralph Waldo Emerson and Walt Whitman and persists throughout the twentieth century in movements like Futurism, Dada, and Fluxus.[6] This is a tradition that affirms the value of attention to the everyday above all else, including art. For Wordsworth, the "discerning intellect" will find paradise in the "simple produce of the common day."[7] Art, including his poetry, is at best a stepping stone to the appreciation of the wonder that surrounds us, a sentiment echoed by Emerson, who writes "painting and sculpture are gymnastics of the eye, its training to the niceties and curiosities of its function. There is no statue like this living man, with his infinite advantage over all ideal sculpture … Away with your nonsense of oil and easels, of marble and chisels: except to open your eyes to the masteries of eternal art, they are hypocritical rubbish."[8]

That is, authentic eternal art is to be found in the everyday and what we call "art" is merely propaedeutic to the aesthetic appreciation of the ordinary. Moreover, if for Wordsworth, the everyday referred to nature, then by the time of Whitman, encouraged by Emerson (whom he called "Master"), it also encompassed the products of the industrial world, of whose modern wonders he sings.[9]

This recuperative project resonates throughout the twentieth century and, in the 1960s in America, it was articulated as the ambition to close the gap, as Robert Rauschenberg put it, between art and life. Judson's and Rainer's preoccupation with everyday movement was of a piece with this moment. But I am not assimilating them to the Wordsworth-Emerson line of thought merely by analogy. There is an actual historical link here, namely the composer John Cage, with whose teachings the relevant choreographers became familiar in classes with Robert Dunn at the Cunningham Studio, which then served as a launching pad for the Judson Dance movement.

6 For a penetrating analysis of this tradition, see George J. Leonard, *Into the Light: The Art of the Commonplace from Wordsworth to John Cage* (Chicago: University of Chicago Press, 1994).

7 William Wordsworth, "Preface to the Edition of 1814," in *The Excursion in Wordsworth: Poetical Works*, Thomas Hutchinson and Ernest De Selincourt, eds. (Oxford: Oxford University Press, 1936), 590.

8 Ralph Waldo Emerson, "Art," *Essays* (Reading, PA: The Spencer Press, 1936), 243.

9 See Walt Whitman, "Passage to India," (especially sections 1 and 2) in *Walt Whitman: The Complete Poems*, Francis Murphy. ed. (London: Penguin Books, 1996), 428 – 29. For commentary, see 134.

Walk, She Said during *This is the story*
of a woman who...
Theater for the New City 1973
original choreography 1972
John Erdman, Yvonne Rainer
photo: Babette Mangolte

opposite:
while shooting *The Man Who Envied*
Women in 1985
Mark Daniels, Yvonne Rainer
photo: Abigail Heyman

Cage, influenced by Zen as well as Emerson, was dedicated to recalling listeners to the glories of ordinary sound. For him the contrast between music and noise was an invidious one he was committed to deconstructing. In *4′ 33″*, perhaps his most discussed work, a pianist enters the hall, sits at the keyboard, opens a score, and then remains silent for four minutes and thirty-three seconds, gradually drawing the audience's attention to ambient sounds, whatever they might be. The pianist's silence functions as a framing device; it alerts listeners to the rich variety of sounds in the room and adjacent spaces. The piece is an attempt to get the audience to listen, to hear afresh the diverse play of the noise of the world and to cherish it.

Similarly, the choreographers of the Judson period were interested in recalling attention to ordinary movement. As Cage strove to dismantle the boundary between music and noise, they attempted to challenge the boundary between dance and ordinary movement for the purpose of kindling an appreciation for that which is generally overlooked. In Rainer's mattress pieces, for example, instead of graceful airs, the viewer is invited to savor the intelligence of human bodies in action as the dancers negotiate moving a heavy and unwieldy object through space. Given this opportunity, framed as it was as a performance, one could only begin to marvel at the precision and subtlety, the bodily *savoir faire* of the human mechanism, which, once defamiliarized by Rainer, finally showed itself forth in a way that reminded us that these very amazements are everywhere around us in the everyday hustle and bustle of the world, where every street is, in effect, a concert hall. This celebration of everyday movement, moreover, continues in Rainer's films where gestures, like the ladling of soup in *MURDER and murder*, are executed with a degree of care and deliberateness that is quite simply arresting.

the transition to film

As is well known, Rainer's interest in film grew out of her desire to examine the emotions more closely. Her focus switched, that is, from a concern with the outer movement of the body to a concern with the inner movement of feeling. Her first feature length film, *Lives of Performers*, is, in effect, what Sally Banes calls a backstage musical.[10] It examines the lives of a group of dancers preparing for a performance of a dance called *Walk, She Said* (the kind of dance Rainer was famous for choreographing). However, in the course of the film, we are not preoccupied with dancing. Instead Rainer attends to the lives, especially in terms of the loves, of the dancers, frequently recounted in dispassionate off-screen monologues and dialogues.

In response to criticisms of Samuel Richardson's novel *Pamela* for dwelling on the representation of domestic life—a topic ostensibly too mundane for and beneath literary attention—Denis Diderot responded that Richardson had achieved something important by redirecting readers' attention to what they generally overlooked, neglected, or took for granted. Similarly, in turning to film, Rainer continued her revolt against modern dance. For rather than presenting dancers as larger-than-life characters, after the fashion of Martha Graham, Rainer brings them down-to-earth, emphasizing that they are quotidian creatures, hesitant, wary, conflicted, desiring, and often confused as they deal with the betrayals, openings, stratagems, and muddles of love (or, at least, sex).[11] Nor is this emotional content treated floridly after the fashion of ballet, modern dance, or even Hollywood. The characters deliver their ruminations about the game of sex in a deadpan, low-key manner far more in keeping with the volume of everyday life and love than the operatic approach that tends to dominate stage and screen. Nevertheless, by examining these relationships, Rainer enters the realm of sexual politics. Employing cinematic references to violence to women in both *Lives of Performers* (where images from Pabst's *Pandora's Box* are

10 Sally Banes, "Dance, Emotion, Film: The Case of Yvonne Rainer," a talk at the symposium on the work of Yvonne Rainer sponsored by the Humanities Institute of New York University in April 1999.

11 For further discussion of *Lives of Performers*, see Noël Carroll, "Moving and Moving: From Minimalism to *Lives of Performers*," in *Millennium Film Journal* 35/36 (Fall 2000), 81–88.

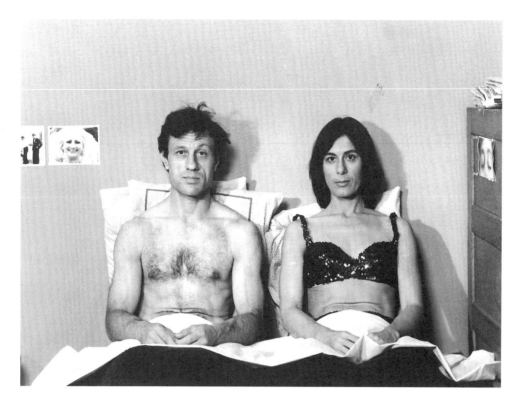

12 The significance of these allusions is
noted by the Camera Obscura
Collective in their "Interview" in
A Woman Who... 158.

restaged) and *Film About A Woman Who...* (which employs stills from the shower scene of Hitchcock's *Psycho*), Rainer broaches the topic of the woman as a victim in patriarchal society.[12] Though hardly programmatic tracts illustrating particular feminist theories, Rainer's early films begin to explore the structures within everyday life, rather than human nature, that support oppression.

In *Film About a Woman Who...*, Rainer examines the everyday anger and rage women feel within the confines of heterosexual relationships. Just as Homer's exposition of Achilles' rage, or *thumos*, in the *Iliad* provides insight to the structure of an entire culture, Rainer's focus on ordinary emotions, particularly women's anger, provides the opportunity to reflect on the daily processes that ensnare women in sexist culture. Their anger becomes a way in which to probe the obstacles that entrammel them.

Women's anger, and its socio-political significance, of course, became a major topic of discussion among feminists in the seventies. And by rehearsing its conditions and velocities, Rainer contributed to the growing conversation about the ways in which everyday life itself can be a source of oppression. With *Film About a Woman Who...*, Rainer turned the recurring themes of the consciousness-raising group, with its emphasis on everyday experience, emotion, and anger, into art.

In *Kristina Talking Pictures*, the theme of everyday life (and everyday sex) as a site of struggle is limned through the extensive readings from Neal Mostert's *Supership*, especially by Raoul, the lion tamer Kristina's lover. This reading brings together an exhaustingly precise description of the organization of everyday life on an oil tanker with political issues, notably the threat of ecological disaster through oil spills. It is as if the break-up between Raoul and the narrator and the breakup of an oil tanker both issue, in socially significant ways, from some structural instability.

Throughout the seventies, Rainer, along with a generation of academics, became increasingly familiar with radical political theory. One radical theme that emerges gradually in her films is the everyday as a site of political struggle, especially with reference to women.[13] For Georg Lukacs, the everyday life of the worker in capitalism provided a perspective from which the oppressiveness of the system could be apprehended. Antonio Gramsci, Henri Lefebvre, and the Situationists theorized the everyday as a terrain upon which resistance to the forces of oppression could be fruitfully waged. Feminism, of course, further specified the terms of engagement as sexual politics. While perhaps not fully conscious of, nor committed to, the pertinent radical theories, Rainer's early films parallel some of their intuitions. On the one hand, by tracking women's victimization in everyday sexual relations, Rainer made available a phenomenological characterization of female oppression. Likewise, by exploring women's rage, Rainer was able to help illuminate the socio-political conditions of everyday life that gave rise to it. Moreover, by her use of disjunctive strategies of exposition, juxtaposition, and collage, Rainer attempted to challenge the blandishments of the culture industry, the alleged source, for many, including Guy Debord, for the degradation of everyday life. Indeed, Rainer, by frequently alluding to and defamiliarizing mass-media imagery, especially movies, cast a critical light on various scenarios that contribute to women's oppression.

is the personal political?

As the 1970s converged on the 1980s, the tenor of intellectual life, especially in the art world and academia, became increasingly theoretical, where "theoretical" in the relevant precincts was virtually synonymous with "political." The ascendancy of such theory, which tended to be politicized poststructuralism and its various, associated jargons, is reflected in Rainer's films *Journeys from Berlin/1971* and *The Man Who Envied*

13 For an overview of radical thinking about the everyday, see John Roberts, "Philosophizing the Everyday: The Philosophy of Praxis and the Fate of Cultural Studies," in *Radical Philosophy*, no. 98 (November/December, 1999), 16 – 29.

14 For a discussion of New Talkies, see Noël Carroll, "Film in the Age of Postmodernism," in Carroll, *Interpreting the Moving Image* (Cambridge: Cambridge University Press, 1998).

Women. Whereas Rainer's relation to explicit political theory in her earlier films is more of the nature of a spiritual affinity or parallel, in these next two films, it becomes more explicit and pronounced. Perhaps one reason for this is that "theory" itself became more a part of the daily life world/art world that Rainer inhabited and used as the basis of her work. Though undoubtedly concerned with the claims of theory, Rainer was also infatuated with its sound as it rubbed against the everyday. However, even if Rainer's work in the first half of the eighties begins to take on a more overtly theoretical/political complexion, it is nevertheless unlike comparable films of the same period—often called New Talkies[14]—that also take on politicized post-structuralism as its content. For the New Talkies, like Laura Mulvey and Peter Wollen's *Riddles of the Sphinx,* tended to use cinema to illustrate the theories that enamored their makers, whereas Rainer presents no unified theory or political viewpoint but rather sets theories and viewpoints in motion in ways that they undercut and question each other, thereby confronting the viewer with issues to think through instead of conclusions.

If Rainer's films are theoretical, they are not so in virtue of delivering and defending finished theories to the audience but in prompting us to think theoretically and practically about the issues, information, and conflicting perspectives on our own. If one finds a theoretical option voiced at one moment in one of Rainer's films, one may be fairly sure that one will later hear down the road some other theory, fact, or consideration that will qualify the easy acceptance of the earlier theory.

One conviction of the late 1970s and early 1980s that Rainer explores in this period is the notion that the personal is political—that everyday life reduces to politics without remainder. In *Journeys from Berlin/1971,* Rainer questions whether all women's oppression and rage is political, a viewpoint attributed to her by some commentators on her early films and, in any event, a cliché among radicals of the time. Through the representation of an extended psychoanalytic therapy of an attempted suicide patient,

played with consummate brio by Annette Michelson, Rainer challenges the equation of inner fury and self-loathing with anything reasonably called politics. And, in the same film, Rainer also interrogates the converse of the proposition that the personal is political viz. the supposition that the political is ultimately personal—that political outrage is reducible to (and dispensable as) mere personal frustration and disappointment. Rainer broaches this issue by reviewing the case of Ulrike Meinhof, whose saga might seem to give some credence to the view that political outrage is nothing but the fury of personal demons. However, then Rainer troubles this conclusion by introducing the case of certain nineteenth-century Russian anarchists whose actions stemmed from a sense of injustice rather than a sense of personal distress. Juxtaposing the cases of the attempted-suicide, of Meinhof, of the Russian anarchists, and of others, Rainer encourages the viewer to contemplate the issues comparatively and contrastively from every angle.[15]

The possible conflictual relationship between the personal and the political is one of the central subjects in Rainer's *The Man Who Envied Women*. The man in question is Jack Deller, an academic who talks "theory-speak" as easily as the proverbial sailor curses. He is politically informed, articulates the "correct" views on every issue, and can effortlessly translate his convictions into prescribed jargon, replete with long, abstract quotations from Michel Foucault et al. Of course, Jack is a feminist. However, we also see that in many ways, in his personal behavior, Jack is also a sexist, though perhaps a genuinely self-deceived one, since he proclaims his great love of women to his psychoanalyst in language that he never realizes is unbearably self-serving and condescending. Jack uses political theory-speak as a means to power and seduction. Nor is he the only person in the intellectual hothouse where he dwells to do so.

One of Rainer's presiding questions in this film appears to be whether the compromised personality of a Lothario like Jack Deller is enough to vitiate the positions he

15 For further discussion of *Journeys From Berlin/1971*, see Noël Carroll, "Introduction to *Journeys From Berlin/1971*," in Carroll, *Interpreting the Moving Image*.

seems to stand for. Does his flawed, finally hypocritical status reflect something deeply wrong in his views (since his words so mismatch his deeds)? Is the everyday world of intellectuals like him merely a sham? Perhaps the knowledge-is-power thesis, so popular with people like Jack Deller, applies ironically to their own use of theory-speak.

Another aspect of everyday life that Rainer raises in *The Man Who Envied Women* is housing, maybe the most daunting problem of daily existence in New York City. Rainer includes documentary footage of public hearings about the Artist/Ownership Project, a plan to turn city-owned property over to artists in order to ensure them a place to live and work. These hearings become quite heated, since the interests of the artistic community are at odds with those of the Hispanic community. Though artists, especially contemporary artists, are prone, almost by reflex, to assume that they are allied with the downtrodden, theory collides with reality during these hearings. The artists, it is suggested, are on the wrong side of the debate; that is, on the side of privilege. Thus Rainer problematizes the unexamined talk of the intellectual milieu of which she is both a participant and an observer. The facile identification of artists and knowledge-workers with and as the oppressed is undermined and another incongruity of the daily existence of artists is brought out into the open by focussing on one of the basic conditions of everyday life: the competition for shelter.

The Man Who Envied Women is possibly Rainer's most popular film. It takes a hard, comic look at the pretensions of artists and intellectuals, and comments astutely on the theoretical excesses of the early eighties. Nevertheless, it is not a brief for abandoning political commitment, but rather a reminder that politics do and should mean something.

recent films

Privilege is a more explicitly feminist film than the early films that won Rainer a reputation as a feminist filmmaker. One of its leading themes is women and aging, especially menopause. It emphasizes how this fact of everyday life is, as one character says, "a well kept secret, something you don't want to know about unless you're a woman past her prime … over the hill … has seen better days…" Moreover, as the indignation evident in this quotation makes clear, this silence is not benign. It is a sign of the position of women in patriarchal society where their youthful bodies are valued, but, as their bodies age, they become marginalized. Menopause, and society's attitude toward this natural state as some sort of disease or flaw, stands as a symptom of society's evaluation of aging women.

Privilege begins with the shooting of a film-within-a-film—a documentary about menopause. But as the filmmaker questions one of her interviewees, Jenny, she has a flashback ("a hot flashback" as she says) to her twenties. This provides Rainer with the opportunity to review the aging process as the older interviewee comments on her younger self and comes to an acute awareness of the degree to which her self-conception is bound up with her body and men's attitude towards it. By identifying oneself with one's body, Rainer indicates that one unconsciously complies with a system of injustices done to the female body, which includes unnecessary hysterectomies and other uncalled for medical (and psychiatric) procedures, sexual harassment and abuse, and even rape. The acceptance by women of this self-identification with the body provides a crucial premise for a system that renders the everyday life of women oppressive in significant ways.

But *Privilege* is not simply about the injustices experienced by aging women. Throughout the eighties, it was a commonplace among artists, intellectuals, and academics not

while shooting *Privilege*
Gabriella Ferrar, Yvonne Rainer
photo: Vivian Selbo

to discuss gender without also addressing race and class. In *Privilege*, Rainer leads with the gender card, using menopause and Jenny's aging as a means of raising issues of sexual injustice. But in the process of her flashback, Jenny also recounts the stories of her neighbors, the Hispanic couple, Carlos and Digna, in the adjacent building, and Brenda, a lesbian who lives on the floor below Jenny. It is through the interaction of these characters that Rainer introduces considerations of race and class. Apparently Carlos attempts to rape Brenda. Race enters the picture here, since Carlos, in accordance with the mores of American culture, considers himself black (black enough to be denied residence in Brenda's building) and racial tension underscores his confrontation with her. At Carlos's trial, Jenny bears false witness against Carlos, alleging that she saw Carlos in Brenda's apartment, although she did not. This leads Digna to comment critically on Jenny's obliviousness to the class dynamics that determined her behavior.

Though *Privilege* engages the trio of race, class and gender, it does it in a way that is very distinctive. Typically, this triad is thought of as a package deal; racism, classism, and sexism are of a piece. The victims of each form a natural alliance, they have a bond with the victims of the others. But in *Privilege*, Rainer stresses that this is too complacent a viewpoint. Jenny, the white woman, has, as the title of the film indicates, a degree of privilege that is not shared with people like Carlos and Digna, and these advantages set her at odds with them in many important ways, ways in which Jenny is unaware. If race, class, and gender are important concepts for analyzing the structures of everyday life, Rainer reminds us that the forces they represent stand in complex and sometimes conflictual relations to each other inasmuch as the victims of daily oppression can also be its agents.

In *MURDER and murder*, Rainer returns to two of the themes of *Privilege*: growing older and the suspicion of the medical establishment. *MURDER and murder* is

primarily the story of two lesbians—one of whom has breast cancer—learning to
negotiate their lives together. Doris is the woman with cancer; she is a performance
artist, spirited and somewhat wary of the relationship, since she has only recently
come to acknowledge her love of women. The other member of the couple is Mildred,
an academic intellectual, very proper in her manner, though deeply affectionate
underneath her seemingly aloof exterior. Although the film has political dimensions,
concerning the rapacity of drug companies and the negligence of society at large
with respect to the death toll women suffer as a result of cancer today, the center of
gravity in *MURDER and murder* is the process through which Doris and Mildred come
to forge their modus vivendi, adjusting their often sharply contrasting personalities
to each other's needs and confronting the awesome threat of cancer.

Of all of Rainer's films, *MURDER and murder* seems to me to be the one that is most
concerned with the dynamics of character psychology. Rainer lavishes a great deal of
attention on observing the ways in which Doris and Mildred misunderstand each
other and on how they attempt to deal with those misunderstandings—both unsuc-
cessfully and successfully—supplying along the way helpful suggestions about how to
express one's feelings and anxieties in less combative ways than couples are apt to do.
MURDER and murder is a love story, but a love story that is consistently alert to the
daily obstacles, everyday disappointments and suspicions, and quotidian conflicts that
call for continued repair from day to day in order for a couple to stay together.
Though the fact that the Doris and Mildred are lesbians is joyously emphasized and
though prejudices against lesbians are acknowledged and discussed, the film's attentiveness to the everyday, ongoing construction of a relationship is relevant, movingly
so, to couples of every sexual orientation. It is true that the film employs one of those
staples of melodrama—the medical catastrophe. But this is not invoked in the strained,
sentimental manner of *Love Story*. Given Doris's age, it is plausible that she might

suffer a major physical crisis, and, in any case, a life-threatening affliction is in the cards for every couple that remains together. It is to Rainer's credit that she is able to capture the tremors and tensions such events occasion so subtly.

If in previous films, Rainer explored the everyday as a site of struggle where the socio-political forces that shape the arena are underlined, in *MURDER and murder* the everyday as a personal site of struggle is given more play. The struggle between Doris and Mildred to live a life harmoniously day by day is symbolized by staging a parodic boxing match between them. Happily, it ends with the two boxers, exhausted, falling to the mat and into each other's arms.

The film proper ends as a title card appears announcing "The Rest of this Life." Doris and Mildred are in the kitchen. They take soup from the stove and sit at table together, making small talk about the meal to the everyday sound of spoons against china. This is a rewarding calm point in the struggle to keep love together— a celebration of the quotidian.

Yvonne Rainer
photo: Martha Gever

skirting and aging: an aging artist's memoir

Yvonne Rainer

*Lecture delivered at the The Doreen B. Townsend Center for the Humanities,
University of California, April 11, 2002*

t o talk about the career of a dancer or choreographer is necessarily, either directly or indirectly, to talk about aging. Graphic artists, musicians, photographers, composers, and writers don't age; they mature. But there is no getting around it that the dancer's physical instrument, her body, grows weaker, stiffer, less supple; it, in a word, ages, and that very fact of physical deterioration, universal to all living things on this earth, will affect the young dancer's future in far more profound ways than that of any other kind of artist.

With that said let me begin by showing a few examples of choreographic work from my young dancer days, work that was part of a much larger cultural movement in the explosive 1960s. By the early sixties the ongoing modernist assault on previous art forms took as its latest targets certain practices that, though radical in their day, had become accepted and downright respectable in critical circles. In music it was Schoenberg and the 12-tone row; in dance it was Martha Graham and Doris Humphrey and the exalted transformation of the performer; in the visual arts it was the Abstract Expressionists and their heroic gestures. All of this was grist for the confrontational mills of the followers of Marcel Duchamp, Merce Cunningham, and John Cage. There ensued a period of exuberant productivity in which dancers walked and ran, painters and sculptors made dances, and composers sat at pianos doing nothing in particular while the audience coughed. In the words of choreographer Simone Forti, "You could say it was an atmosphere of 'anything goes.' But that 'anything' had to come from a clear source of longing or inspiration."

[*Dance slides shown here.*]

That's a small sampling of the public side of my career. But there is an equally important private side which I'm going to share with you. It must have been sometime in 1985 that I bragged to a friend "I'm no longer afraid of men." I hadn't trucked sexually

Satie for Two
studio photo 1962
Yvonne Rainer, Trisha Brown
costumes by James Waring

with "them" for at least four years—I was fifty years old—and it would be another five years before I would venture into intimacy with a woman, although I had already begun to call myself a "political lesbian." The question continues to vex me as to why I spent so many years fooling around with what now seem to have been preordained doomed heterosexual partnerships. Though the answers are as numerous as the day is long, I'll confine myself to one in particular, and that is that until the late eighties, I was more attuned to heterosexual feminism than to the gay rights movement and therefore was not given, or could not give myself, permission to tune in to another level of desire.

But it hadn't always been that way. My first "liberation" came at age eighteen when I moved out of my parents' house in San Francisco across the bay to Berkeley. While browsing in a bookstore, the most beautiful woman I had ever seen struck up a conversation with me. Tim was twenty-five, a graduate student in psychology at UC Berkeley, and bisexual. She took me to her house, told me her life story, talked about her conquests. I fell in love. Tim was worldly-wise, wore Navajo jewelry, had studied modern dance, could discuss anything and everything, had an IQ of 165 (so she said) and long, flowing black hair. (I had chopped off my hair bowl-fashion shortly after falling in with some socialist Zionists from Hashomer Hatzair in my third year in high school.) Although we slept in the same bed, she refused to make love to me, her reason being that she didn't want the responsibility. I confided to her that the woman in my sexual fantasies looked like Marilyn Monroe or Jayne Mansfield. She said that a woman like that would probably want someone more butch than me. It was 1953.

The foregoing anecdote can be further situated in its proper historical context when I confess that shortly thereafter I got myself picked up by an ex-GI in a North Beach bar, thereby unwittingly launching a life of compulsive (no less than compulsory)

Trio A
Portland Center for Visual Arts 1973
original choreography 1966
Yvonne Rainer

heterosexuality. It cannot be said often enough that, for a young woman in 1953, everything in the culture militated toward pleasing men.

By 1970 I was reading *Sisterhood is Powerful*, Valerie Solanis's *Scum Manifesto*, and Shulamith Firestone's *The Dialectics of Sex*. Excerpts from Firestone's analysis of romantic love still read with a burning clarity:

Thus "falling in love" is no more than the process of alteration of male vision—idealization, mystification glorification—that renders void the woman's class inferiority. However, the woman knows that this idealization, which she works so hard to produce, is a lie, and that it is only a matter of time before he "sees through her." Her life is a hell, vacillating between an all-consuming need for male love and approval to raise her class subjection, to persistent feelings of inauthenticity when she does achieve his love. Thus her whole identity hangs in the balance of her love life. She is allowed to love herself only if a man finds her worthy of love.[1]

Yes, it was the light from *his* eyes as I described the making of *Trio A*—the dance that was to become my signature piece—that first illuminated my achievement. This may have taken place in Monte's, or maybe the San Remo, in the Village, over double vodka martinis in the winter of 1965. I watched his expression change from polite attention to intense appreciation, even wonderment, as I described the details of creation. I was saved.

Firestone's recasting of Freud and Marx and Solanis's apocalyptic vision did more than fuel my outrage at private and patriarchal, imagined and real, oppression. Their writings—and those of a welter of other feminists—gave me permission to begin examining my experience as a woman, as an intelligent and intelligible participant in culture and society rather than the overdetermined outcome of a lousy childhood that had previously dominated my self-perception. (I should add that at this point, in the

1 Shulamith Firestone, *The Dialectics of Sex: The Case for Feminist Revolution* (New York: Morrow Quill Paperback, 1970), 132.

He presses his face and chest
against the wall. He gives
way, without shame, to a fit of
uncontrollable sobbing.

early seventies, the debates around the competing definitions of "woman"—as biological entity, mythical archetype, or social construction—were barely on the horizon.) I began to come of age reading this stuff. Change, of course, comes with greater difficulty than the reading of a couple of books. The struggle to throw off the status of unknowing collaborator in victimization—at both ends of the domination scale—is uneven and ongoing. But after 1971 my work began to reflect with ever more confidence the details of daily life and social implications of "being a woman" in a white middle-class culture.

I made a transition from choreography to filmmaking between 1972 and 1975. In a general sense my burgeoning feminist consciousness was an important factor. An equally urgent stimulus was the physical changes encroaching on my aging body. But I can also attribute the change in medium, from moving body to moving image, to the emotional power of Hollywood melodramas and European art films seen from a very early age, plus the films of Maya Deren, Hollis Frampton, and Andy Warhol viewed in the early and late sixties. Against this multifarious background of 1) Vigo, Renoir, Cocteau, Dreyer, Pabst and "women's weepies" and 2) the formal strategies of the avant-garde, I intuited that I was venturing into a mother lode of possibility.

Emotions are the repressed detritus of life in the public sphere. There they regularly erupt, with varying degrees of credibility, in news stories, theatrical dramatizations, and television's "real time." From wrestling matches, reports of murder and terrorist attacks to Shakespeare and *One Life to Live*, we have become accustomed to the vicarious experience of phatic extremity.

In the 1960s the nuts and bolts of emotional life comprised the unseen (or should I say "unseemly"?) underbelly of high Minimalism in the U.S. While some of us aspired to the lofty and cerebral plane of a quotidian materiality, our unconscious lives

We Shall Run
Wadsworth Atheneum 1965
original choreography 1963
Yvonne Rainer, Deborah Hay, Robert
Rauschenberg, Robert Morris, Sally Gross,
Joseph Schlichter, Tony Holder, Alex Hay
photo: Peter Moore
© Estate of P. Moore/VAGA, NYC

skirting and aging: an aging artist's memoir

WAR
Loeb Student Center,
New York University 1970
photo: Peter Moore
© Estate of P. Moore/VAGA, NYC

title appearing at the beginning of
Lives of Performers (16mm film, 1972)
and as projected text in
This is the story of a woman who...
text by Leo Bersani

Cliché is, in a sense, the purest art of intelligibility; it tempts us with the possibility of enclosing life within beautifully inalterable formulas, of obscuring the arbitrary nature of imagination with the appearance of necessity.

unraveled with an intensity and melodrama that inversely matched their absence in the boxes, portals, and jogging of our austere creations.

By 1973 my own private sturm und drang had catapulted me into a new terrain of representation. As a survivor of various physical and psychic traumas, and emboldened by the women's movement, I felt entitled to struggle with an entirely new lexicon. The language of specific emotional experience, already familiar outside the avant-garde art world, in drama, novels, cinema, and soap opera, promised all the ambivalent pleasures of the experiences themselves: seduction, passion, rage, betrayal, terror, grief, and joy.

However, the terms, or formal conditions, of this new world would remain tied to the disjunctive and aleatory procedures that had laid claim to my earliest development as an artist. In a nutshell, this mindset can be characterized by a refusal of narrative, by a deep distrust of the "telling" and shaping strategies of fiction and history, and, contrarily, by a refusal to pretend that the world speaks itself. But more about this later.

Some of my dances had contained specific political references; during the Vietnam War, for instance, when they also incorporated language. But to deal more directly with the specifics of emotional life, which was what I set out to do as I began to inch toward film, was such a novel enterprise that I had to find justification in literary criticism for what felt like clichéd and stereotyped expression. It was Leo Bersani's observations about cliché that offered me the support I needed.

Inner Appearances of 1971 became the first section of a multimedia theater piece titled *This is the story of a woman who...*, which was originally performed by John Erdman, Shirley Soffer, and me at the Theater for the New City in New York in the spring of 1973. Chronologically it lies between the dances and films, but it also bridges the

The face of this character is a fixed mask. We shall have her wear an eye shade to reveal her inner and outer appearance. The eye shade hides the movement of the upper half of her face, but the lower half, where the tongue works, stays visible. She must function with a face of stone and at the same time reveal her characteristic dissembling.

voice-over narration in
Lives of Performers
and projected text in
This is the story of a woman who...

2 Vladimir Nizhny, *Lessons with Eisenstein* (New York: Hill & Wang, 1962), 9.

abstractions and "radical juxtapositions" of dance and the emotional specificities, linkages, and obligations of narrative.

In *Inner Appearances* a solitary performer, initially myself, dressed in casual pants and shirt and an old-fashioned green printer's eye shade, alternated everyday actions, from slowly and meditatively vacuuming the floor to turning off the vacuum cleaner, lying down on a mattress, or standing, apparently lost in thought. Behind the performer appeared a sequence of texts on a white wall dealing with the inner thoughts of a female protagonist who was designated only by third-person pronouns. In later performances the projected texts were adapted for a male protagonist simply by substituting male pronouns for the female.

This work can be seen as an exercise in psychological attribution, a first step in a twenty-five year trajectory from performer to persona, from everyday movement to illusionist narrative, a journey that was never without ambivalence and misgiving and would necessarily force me to constantly reassess conventions of fictional authenticity.

[*The first projection in the piece was the text shown above.*]

This is a paraphrase, extracted from a description of a film workshop conducted by Sergei Eisenstein in which he discussed how Balzac characterizes Mademoiselle Michonneau in *Le Pere Goriot*.[2] The paragraph seemed to encapsulate perfectly both dilemma and solution of the narrative conundrum. If the unmoving human facial exterior gave up neither interpretation nor meaning, and visual representation belied human interiority, the "inner and outer appearance" of a performer could be nudged toward a *semblance* of coherence and "sense" by very minimal means indeed. In an epiphany of revelation, I appropriated Eisenstein's eye shade and text and proceeded to deploy the standard form of anecdotal third-person narrative writing to create a disjunctive sequence of memories, events, and feelings. The spatial and temporal contiguity of performer and texts would, hopefully, produce not an illusion of character and authentic history, but something in that vicinity, something provisional and surprising, even unsettling, perhaps something that might call into question what narrative traditionally accomplishes. In the words of Hayden White, "... narrativity ... arises out of a desire to have real events display the coherence, integrity, fullness, and closure of an image of life that is and can only be imaginary."[3] In the embarrassing wars around prospecting for proxies of experience, I was ever on the lookout for strategies that would evade the siren calls of that desire and its unacknowledged, or unconscious, acting out.

At the same time, paradoxically and a little naïvely, I rejoiced in the potential of "visualized text"—read simultaneously and communally in the dark by the theater audience—to induce a *frisson* similar to the effect of a monologue delivered by a great actor. Print, because it was eschewed by traditional theatrical practice, would "defamiliarize" the clichés of enacted emotional excess and make them fresh. The words, isolated from a social or characterological context, and coexisting with a task-involved figure, would in and of themselves cause a quickening in those who read them in the darkened theater. Or so I hoped.

Brechtian notions of alienation and distanciation had already infused the work of The Living Theater and Richard Foreman, which I had followed throughout the sixties. I would now embark on bringing a version of these techniques to the representation of episodes in my own checkered past, events that would be fictionalized through narrative fragmentation, text/image combinations, and uninflected delivery of lines designed to invoke but not replicate the familiar rhetoric and role-playing of disaffected love. These were my guidelines when I assayed a first 16mm feature film in 1972.

Some people have called those early films of mine "pre-political" or "pre-feminist." In fact, *Film About a Woman Who...* of 1974 became a focal point for more than one

3 Hayden White, "The Value of Narrativity in the Representation of Reality," *Critical Inquiry* 7 (Autumn 1980), 24.

Events of the past rose like waves and, battering against her mind, threw it into a wild commotion of shame, grief, and joy.

projected text
This is the story of a woman who...
and title in
Film About a Woman Who...
(16mm film, 1974)

opposite:
Inner Appearances
Theater for the New City
1973
original choreography 1971
photo: Peter Moore
© Estate of P. Moore/VAGA, NYC

brouhaha in the feminist film theory wars of the late seventies and early eighties. The battles raged over issues of positive versus negative imaging of women, avant-garde versus Hollywood, strategies of distanciation versus traditional tactics of identification, elitism versus populism, documentary versus fiction, accessibility versus obscurity, etc. etc. I sometimes found myself fending off partisans from both sides of the barricades.

And now at last I return to the topic with which I began by showing a clip from a film released in 1990 that evolved initially out of my experience with menopause, and in the process became an investigation into the implications of social privilege in the areas of race and gender.

[*Clip from* Privilege *is shown.*]

poster with image from *Privilege*
Gabriella Farrar and other cast and
crew members
Kunsthalle Wien 2001

SABINE FOLIE: The starting point for including Yvonne Rainer in the exhibition *A Baroque Party* was her 1996 film *MURDER and murder:* hardly any other contemporary work of art brings together so many elements of baroque rhetoric. *MURDER and murder* is, if you will, a baroque didactic poem *(Lehrgedicht)*. The narrative, based on the artist's biography, tells the story of two women in their sixties who develop a love relationship. One of them is a performance artist, the other is a Women's Studies professor. The performer gets breast cancer. *MURDER and murder* then, is at the same time the love story of a lesbian couple and a very personal research into the socio-political and economic implications of an enormously widespread disease among women. It's an examination and denunciation of medical and political neglect and of the current state of sexual politics, discrimination, etc. The rather dry and rational way that statistical facts are delivered by the narrator Yvonne Rainer (in a tuxedo) has a distancing effect. The documentary report creeps into the seemingly traditional narrative of the film and produces a strongly distancing moment in this tragicomedy, exactly in the sense of a baroque polemic. All the types of everyday text production and incidental poetry—such as funeral orations, letters or leaflets—are, incidentally, an integral component of baroque rhetoric. Rainer mediates different rhetorical techniques, "texts" over and next to each other, recently an experimental practice of the avant-garde. This means that contrary to the ancient, extremely formal rhetoric, art and artificiality find their way into life and vice versa.

We have in *MURDER and murder* a literal baroque rhetorical situation like we see, for example, in the poetry of Milton, Gryphious, Ronsard, or, as Lowry Nelson says *(Baroque Lyric Poetry,* 1961), a "complex and dynamic relationship between speaker, audience, and reader." In comparison to Renaissance poetry there are more dramatic elements like "assertions, questions, and exclamations: particularization of time and place; repetition and emphasis," and also elements like "opposite and alternative."

frame enlargement
MURDER and murder (16mm film, 1996)
Kathleen Chalfant and Joanna Merlin

opposite:
Act, a section of *The Mind is a Muscle*
Anderson Theater 1968
Yvonne Rainer, Steve Paxton, David
Gordon, Barbara Dilley, William Davis,
Becky Arnold
photo: Peter Moore
© Estate of P. Moore/VAGA, NYC

I mean to say that these elements are genuine baroque "inventions" or at least very conscious uses of ancient baroque rhetoric. They have a strong affinity with Rainer's montage/collage technique, the infiltration of documentary footage into her films, to say nothing of the moments of masquerade and disguise. The tenor of the piece is theatrical and the mode of expression is baroque, namely rhetorical-dialectical. A street ballad (*Moritat*) is told by means of dialogues between the actors and the spectators and through the direct address of the "director" to the audience about the beautiful and ugly sides of life, using all the formal strategies of meta-narration.

The spectator is to be persuaded by *eloquenzia*. Rainer has made a piece that has, like in the Baroque, an intention to affect, an intention to instruct, to influence, and to move. *Movere, persuadere, flectere, docere, delectare* is the rhetorical (baroque) credo. Buchner, a baroque critic, says that poetry and theater have to instruct and entertain: both aspects are fulfilled in Rainer's film.

PEGGY PHELAN: This is a very rich way to approach *MURDER and murder*. It helps open up some of the richest aspects of the film, and indeed, of Rainer's work more generally. Part of what is surprising to me about your approach is that it sidesteps the usual art-historical categories that still frame much of the critical discussion of Rainer's art work. I am thinking especially of the categories "Minimalism" and "Feminism." When Rainer was working with the other artists of the Judson Dance Theater (Steve Paxton, Trisha Brown, et al.) in the early 1960s, she was choreographing and dancing pieces that were extremely dense—perhaps not so much in terms of movement as such—historically, politically, and to my mind, but not to everyone else's, psychologically. In her famous "No Manifesto," Rainer wrote: "no to movement and being moved." This was taken to be a Minimalist stance, a stripping away of the conventional ideological approach to dance since Balanchine, the investment in pre-supposing psychological depth in "character," the configuration of plot, the synchron-

ic imperative of matching musical score to bodily gesture, and so on. And of course this is accurate, as far as it goes. But what was also at play in Rainer's manifesto, and in her work at the time, was a very curious, indeed layered and perhaps even baroque attitude toward the address created between dancer and spectator. This density has often been addressed in terms of "the male gaze," especially in relation to *Trio A*. But let's return to that dance more fully later.

Here, I just want to point out that what the critical framework of the baroque, as against Minimalism, allows us to expose is the complexity of Rainer's relationship to the address between performer and viewer, a relationship that continues to preoccupy her all through her film work, and reaches an intense concentration in *MURDER and murder*.

I agree with all you say about the film, and would simply like to amplify your remarks about the intermixing of rhetorical forms in the films. I like your comments because they are so attentive to the formal features of her work. Additionally, I just want to note that and the range of intertexts she includes here also extend to the Keystone Cops, in that very funny scene by the elevator before the party. Also, for me, the over-all address of the film proliferates and reproduces itself in an almost chemical way; that is, I think the film is not only about cancer, but that it also mimics some parts of what we have come to believe—even if we still cannot know certainly—about the ways in which cancerous cells divide and replicate. So the film moves both backward and forward, the narrative both projects a future and is "stamped out" in various ways. The precise deconstruction of the intermixing of the chemical companies who both pollute and "cure," for example, reflects something of the toxic nature of cancerous cells themselves. I am not suggesting that Rainer set out to try to make a film that borrows the techniques of cancer, but I am trying to suggest that part of

what happens with Rainer's work is that her subject matter informs her formal choices to a surprising degree, and that there is a kind of dogged literalism to some of her work. This literalism allows her work to cohere, to not spin out into so many directions that the viewer gets lost.

My own understanding of baroque rhetoric is that it flowers. I think Rainer is a careful gardener, and like Florio, for example, she prunes to make the buds more vital.

SABINE FOLIE: That's a beautiful metaphor. Yes, Yvonne Rainer employs her rhetorical means in well-measured doses, with intellectual distance and at the same time empathy. But I have my doubts as to whether this baroque rhetoric will "flower." I think that the images produced, the improvised formulations would actually like to do that, but that the counterbalance that the rhetorical form professes is highly structured. But you also allude to the fact that baroque rhetoric as a discipline is always falling into disfavor, with its methods that seek to convince at all costs and using all means of exaggeration—methods that appear suspicious to a growing bourgeoisie in an empirical époque. I think that these means are every bit as intentional as Rainer's inter-textual language. That's why I find your observation that subject matter influences formal decisions intriguing. I hadn't thought about it, but that suits Rainer's structural approach; and here I would like once more to underscore the importance of Rainer's balancing of form and rhizomatic content.

The pronounced attentiveness that Rainer grants to the relationship between actor and viewer, in contrast to the Minimalist maxim, can be seen in the early dance pieces like *Trio A*, at that time in much more ambivalent ways than is the case in *MURDER and murder*, for example. But even then, Rainer couldn't simply be tucked away into a simple category. She developed an anti-rhetorical rhetoric, in which she sought to withhold the voyeuristic gaze and the attribution of character by technical means,

while shooting *MURDER* and *murder*
Joanna Merlin performs Doris's schtick
photo: Esther Levine

opposite:
frame enlargement
MURDER and *murder*
Yvonne Rainer

which we will discuss later. At the same time, she recognized that "being seen" is unavoidable. For me, and here I completely agree with you, the psychological dimension is also unforeseeable, which is why I will later take issue with affects. But let me be more precise: I would like to underscore, in the sense of Roland Barthes, that I mean a rhetorical psychology, not an abstracting one like we see in the contemporary psychoanalytic sense, in which the figures conceal what seems to be hidden. "What I mean is, I have to signify what I want to be *for the other.*" (Roland Barthes, *The Semiological Adventure*)

Perhaps I can make a quick remark about my non-Minimalist and non-feminist approach to interpretation. I take these means of interpretation for granted, and I could add very little to them, at most extend to them a reductionist, namely baroque focus, although of course my intention is to open the work rather than close it down. I am aware of the danger of juxtaposing a past period with avant-garde art, which has its roots in the past after all, perhaps more than one would think. I wouldn't say that Rainer's work is postmodern because it falls back, consciously or unconsciously, on this visual and mental reservoir. Rainer's work is of course not baroque, but the baroque—which is after all the theme of this exhibition—puts a wealth of congenial traditions and aesthetic practices at our disposal.

Let's come back to *MURDER and murder*. As we already mentioned, the narrator, played by Yvonne Rainer, introduces a kind of "play within a play" into this already multilayered piece of narration, talking to oneself and flashback. She integrates facts and statistics into the already existing narrative: realism as the disillusionment of dreams, the play, and fiction.

The Baroque period was fascinated by the idea of the world as theater, a stage onto which every individual became an actor. In the theatrum mundi of various poets such

as Calderón de la Barca, Cervantes, Shakespeare, or of the stoic philosopher Balthasar Gracián, this role is not necessarily determined. Rather, the protagonist becomes merely a "persona," when s/he acts out all the possibilities life has to offer.

The baroque theatrum mundi is not just theater, but rather a celebration of a radical "being in the world." It is reality, not fiction, and death always looms in the background. The world is a theater; therefore a theater performance is a play within a play and the actors are comfortable being the play things of illusion and disillusion. The more they are entranced by illusion, the more the benevolent face brings its horrible, grotesque and deadly shadow side into view. Masks and emphatic gestures emphasize the grotesque and sometimes macabre play, as we see in *MURDER and murder*, but everyone has to go on stage and experience reality.

MURDER and murder is a comic and grisly fairy tale. Death plays a decisive role: Rainer in her role as the narrator seems to embody Author, God, and Death all at once; she comments on the goings-on, simultaneously distant and sympathetic but not necessarily all-powerful and authoritarian. Rainer in her tuxedo is the moral authority, the warning voice, especially when she reveals her mastectomized chest—a sort of vanitas symbol, a sign of physical and mental pain, of suffering bodies—and when she contrasts the scene at the same time with a humorous and sarcastic slapstick. In this way, reality doesn't become pathetic but rather even more real. There is room for empathy, but not for sentimentality. We only need to think again about the scene that you already mentioned, the one by the elevator at the so-called party.

Satire, burlesque moments, the (baroque) revue of fools, all of these things show that life is tragic and comic at the same time. The characters at the party in Rainer's film present their roles before the audience (the gods) and you would have to laugh if you weren't so unsure that you shouldn't cry instead. These moments of slapstick and

vaudeville humor allow the spectator to accept and to experience the unbearable truth, reality. It is in these moments of the play/the fiction that reality shows itself so movingly and persuasively.

"Speaking is acting" is a baroque motto. "Dancing is acting" could be Rainer's motto for her early dance pieces and films. There is also dance in *MURDER and murder*, a calculated yet seemingly arbitrary movement in space.

Dancing is speaking is acting. All these elements form the dense and interwoven language in Yvonne Rainer's work: the dance as gesture, as a movement of affects.

PEGGY PHELAN: This is all very inspiring! I think you are investigating a very rich and useful approach to Rainer's work. Your paraphrase of the baroque motto "speaking is acting" resonates for me with what might, at first glance, seem like the opposite sentiment, i.e., Jacques Lacan's axiom, "To speak is to suffer." I think of this because of your remarks about the presence of death, its clinging nearness, in the work of artists and philosophers we associate with the theatrum mundi. In Shakespeare, this might seem a bit hard to contemplate since there is such obvious exuberance about the capacity to speak, especially on public stages like The Globe, the architectural version of the theatrum mundi. But the other side of this exuberance—indeed perhaps the force that propels the exuberance—is the consciousness of speech ending. (The theaters were often forced to close for all sorts of reasons, thus silencing theatrical speech, and death was often quick and frequent in the plays themselves.) For Calderón and Cervantes, the thing that propelled their rhetoric was the intensity of the need to dream, especially because fear of death was what otherwise kept them up at night. Part of what I think Rainer demonstrates vividly in *MURDER and murder* is that the speaking about cancer, the density of its rhetoric—metastasis, chemo, slash and burn, mastectomy, lumpectomy, radical mastectomy—causes even the healthy to suffer. To

production still
MURDER and murder
Kathleen Chalfant, Joanna Merlin,
Yvonne Rainer
photo: Esther Levine

e-mail correspondence between sabine folie and peggy phelan

speak of cancer is not only to suffer the awareness of death but also to feel the limit of the signifier—the inability to "cure" cancer, and the impossibility of conveying precisely how the incapacity to speak one's dread perpetuates a kind of psychological toxicity akin to cancer's own.

Much of this can be said about any cancer; the particular force of breast cancer activates common anxieties many women feel about speaking within phallogocentric culture. While it is the case that men also sometimes are afflicted with breast cancer, the preponderance of cases occur in women. My point here is that when considering Rainer's work in relation to the baroque it is useful to think about where the baroque continues to exert a contemporary force; one such place might be in the rhetorical densities of the discourse of cancer. This discourse is itself haunted by death, and as with the artists we associate with the theatrum mundi, its elaborate structure sets itself as a protection against death's encroachment.

It is useful also, I think, to consider *MURDER and murder* as a sophisticated continuation of Rainer's interest in dance. You mention the performance of dancing throughout the film, but the extension is not only literal at the level of subject matter. ("Once she was a choreographer and dancer and now she makes films in which characters dance.") When I referred to Rainer's "dogged literalism" earlier, I was thinking of one of her early dance pieces called *Move*, in which dancers moved mattresses and other heavy items to frame all the movement central to the task of moving one's home.

Similarly, if we think of dance as movement, Rainer's films are themselves moving pictures—or indeed as we often say in English—"movies." The play of light both in the scene and in the projector move in such a way that we can see the dancer dancing. In the wonderful boxing scene, in which the lovers move in and out of the ring, in

and out of falling and rising, embracing and hurting each other, we can read, on the canvas floor of the ring, a series of statistics tracking a different kind of battle from the one we are watching in the boxing ring. This juxtaposition sutures both kinds of information together in what I think you must be right to call a baroque manner.

It is also interesting to recall that in your description of the party, in which the guests present themselves to the audience, whom you call "Gods," echoes of Rainer's past work can be heard. For example, in her late theater piece of 1970, *Grand Union Dreams*, a piece she made upon her return from India and just before she began making her long films, some of the performers are indeed cast as gods. I think this kind of allusion is perhaps subtle, especially if one is unaware of Rainer's earlier work, but I point it out in the spirit of the rhizome. If I am to be a gardener here, I'd like to know how deep the roots of what I'm pruning really are.

SABINE FOLIE: Your comments on the connection between Lacan and the poets of the theatrum mundi produce a vivid image of the topic we are dealing with here. They allow us to see the dialectical and paradoxical position of a concept of survival through poetry and art in general. We know from the mystic Jakob Böhme that a coin always has two sides and that we can only achieve knowledge of the one if we perceive the other as well. This leads to transcendental realism, which was therefore celebrated in the Baroque.

By the way, I also believe that we must emphasize the film's focus on women, in as much as Rainer represents a radical feminism with political acumen (a baroque polemic), intellectual clarity and liberating humor and self-irony.

If we make a plea to bring the baroque into this exhibition as an aesthetic concept, we don't in any way want to interpret Rainer's work in a way that would reduce its

OBJECTS	DANCES
	eliminate or minimize

OBJECTS	DANCES
1. role of artist's hand	phrasing
2. hierarchical relationship of parts	development and climax
3. texture	variation: rhythm, shape, dynamics
4. figure reference	character
5. illusionism	performance
6. complexity and detail	variety: phrasing and the spatial field
7. monumentality	the virtuosic movement feat and the fully-extended body

substitute

OBJECTS	DANCES
1. factory fabrication	energy equality and "found" movement
2. unitary forms, modules	equality of parts
3. uninterrupted surface	(discrete events or repetition)
4. non-referential forms	neutral performance
5. literalness	task or task-like activity
6. simplicity	singular action, event, or tone
7. human scale	human scale

richness and diversity. Rather, the aim is to keep in mind that not all avant-garde practices are new inventions, but that there are genuine, experimental and even radical traditions in the baroque; we would claim, more so in the baroque than in the bourgeois ninetheenth century.

One more word about your remarks on dance in *MURDER and murder* and on the moving images that are literally *tableaux vivants* in Rainer's films, like in *The Man Who Envied Women* or even more so in *Lives of Performers*.

Let's make a somewhat abrupt shift to the other works in the exhibition. That would be to a performance from 1972, *Inner Appearances*, in which Rainer vacuums a room that contains various props—the props are actually not only objects but also a kind of mute protagonist in the room. I told Yvonne Rainer that the situation in this room reminded me of some of the interiors from Samuel Beckett's television plays, and also of the interiors in Vermeer: the chair, the mattress, the gun, the opened letter, the suitcase. The objects are arranged in the space like an animated still life. In our exhibition, there will only be the objects and a text from a "she" and a "he" projected on the wall, without performers. But since Rainer has herself written a text about exactly this work, I would rather delve more deeply into *Trio A*.

What does *Trio A, The Mind is a Muscle, Part 1* (1966) have to do with the baroque? A dance in Minimalist aesthetic, Rainer herself describes her approach for a new dance in her text *The Mind is a Muscle*.

So, every attempt at classical phrasing, expression, metaphor, etc. should be avoided. In fact, the dance as I saw it for the first time in the filmed version produced by Sally Banes (1978) can clearly be called Minimalist. In an empty, black-and-white space Rainer performs an endless loop of movements, a continuum of non-hierarchical figures, although they cannot be called "figures" in the sense of classical rhetoric.

This is the story of a woman who...
Theater for the New City 1973
John Erdman and Yvonne Rainer
photo: Babette Mangolte

opposite:
original manuscript for "A Quasi Survey
of Some 'Minimalist' Tendencies in
the Quantitatively Minimal Dance Activity
Midst the Plethora, or an Analysis of
Trio A," published in *Minimal Art,
A Critical Anthology*, Gregory Battcock,
ed., New York: E. P. Dutton, 1968

Nevertheless, I experience Rainer in general and especially in this dance as a "rhetorical performer," as you once put it.

In a baroque sense, one could speak of affects in the movement. It would probably be an exaggeration to speak of "pathos formulas" in Aby Warburg's sense: gestures of expression, invented in antiquity, occasionally rising to the surface to be taken up again, especially in the Renaissance. And I would add, although Warburg would have protested, also in the baroque. These gestures are of an iconographic nature, but they are also a part of our cultural reservoir, and I would almost say that they are anthropological gestures appropriated from other cultures. If the assumption is not too daring, I'd like to say that these gestures of expression in Rainer's *Trio A* seem to be always interrupted, but are nevertheless resonant. They are exchanged like glances, they remind one of something familiar, buried, remote and are lost again in the next moment.

Warburg speaks of the mythical origins of some trivialized figures and attitudes in our modern commercial world. He tries in his *Mnemosyne Atlas* (1929) to offer proof that gestures and forms that were invented in antiquity are still valid today. These formulas comprise the whole range of the psychological drama: fear, pain, melancholia, joy, escape, persecution, flight, dance, dialogue, the muses, flying, only to cite a few of the categories out of Warburg's atlas.

I think that *Trio A* is affected or animated by an anti-rhetorical rhetoric of passion; this concept would coincide with Rainer's "shared emotion" as an integral part of her work. And the body is the conveyor of this sensation, or as Rainer says, "My body remains the enduring reality."

PEGGY PHELAN: Yes, Rainer was onto herself, and to the main themes of her life's work, early on. Her body remains the enduring reality, but as we have seen with

Trio A
Nova Scotia School of Art and Design 1973
original choreography 1966

MURDER and murder, what that body stages—from the blooms of love late in life to the proliferation of cancer cells and their medico-rhetorical toxicities—changes radically. I think these two truisms—the body endures and the body changes—create two different "figures," both of which we might touch by coming closer to *Trio A*. I think that the endurance/transformation complex informs our sense of what I might call here, albeit a little too broadly, "the psychic self" and "the embodied self." Neither phrase is perfect, but perhaps they will help convey what I mean. To say we are figured by our body and that our psychic, or inner life, informs that figure, is to hint at the doubleness at work in embodiment itself. There is both continuity (Rainer's "enduring reality") and disruption in our apprehension of embodiment and interiority. Thus, we "remember" earlier gestures of our own when we observe an infant, and we remember them both physically and psychologically. These memories are "enduring," but when we see different infants our re-encounter with ourselves is transformed. They are and are not the same memories. So when we speak of Warburg's "pathos formulas" it is important to note that in regard to dance and movement performance, the figures are embodied as well as represented. This is a fundamental difference in the affective force of dance and painting.

That said, however, I very much like the links you make between *Inner Appearances* and Dutch still life painting on the one hand, and Beckett on the other. Much of Beckett's work, especially the late dramas and teleplays, attempted to drain away rhetorical "excess" to arrive at the distillation of existence itself. Not surprisingly, much of this work approaches dance. *Quad* for example is a kind of human chess game, but it is also an inquiry into the way walking is and is not fundamentally self-expressive. (Hence, Beckett's insistence on the uniformity of the blank costumes, and the precise timing and pacing of the steps and why he wanted the same piece performed with and without music.)

frame enlargement
Journeys From Berlin/1971
(16mm film, 1980)

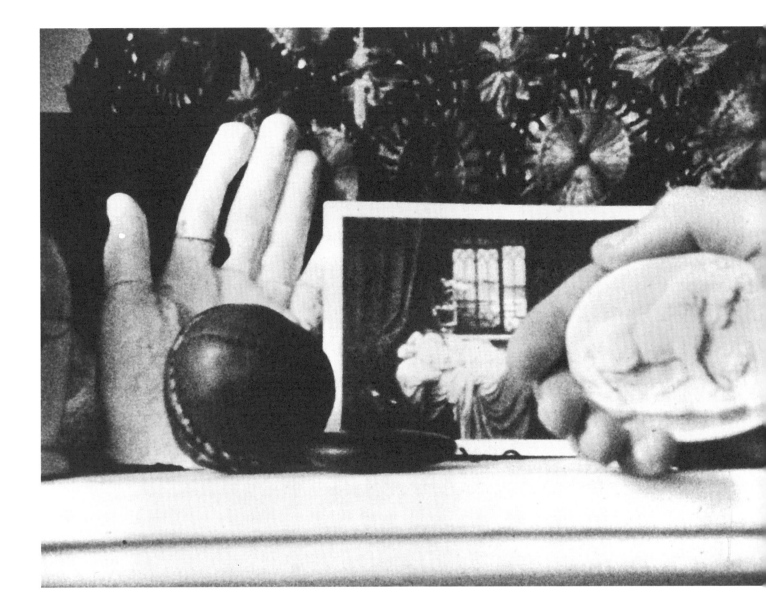

e-mail correspondence between sabine folie and peggy phelan

Rainer was attempting to choreograph pieces for what she called "the neutral doer" at the time she made *Trio A*. Not only did she have the performer avert the gaze, she also, and perhaps for me more interestingly now, eliminated the pose altogether. The pose, among other things, stills movement. There is a kind of resting place, or indeed a glimpse of inanimation, in the midst of most classical dance performances. In *Trio A*, no such stopping point exists. It is as if the piece attempts to make the moving muscles into a melody that is both internal and external. Moreover, by eliminating this stillness, *Trio A* also seems to sidestep a kind of death drive (Freud referred to inanimation itself as a harbinger of the death drive) by insisting on continuous movement. Of course, if we used some of our new high speed visual technologies, we could detect certain seconds of stillness; gravity is a great stopper, for one. But in live performance, such pauses are impossible to discern. While this aspect of the dance has been discussed frequently in terms of its powerful subversion of the apparatus of the male gaze, in retrospect, this refusal to be still interests me.

It is as if Rainer understood, and feared, the drive toward "the still life" in dance itself. This is why I like your connection to the Dutch masters. You mention Rainer's use of props in the piece, and connect it to the *tableau vivants* in *The Man Who Envied Women*. Yes, although interestingly, the objects to which Rainer's camera continually returns in that film are the photographs on the wall. Most of them come from magazines. As still photographs within the ongoing movement of the film, they function as a touchstone of the "enduring reality" of the film's visual body, and each time the camera returns to them, they are re-framed and re-encountered via the voice-over commentaries about them, especially those of Martha Rosler. In other words, in *The Man Who Envied Women*, the camera returns to the wall photographs to consider how images have been framed by other cameras. This is a different activity from the similar returns to the objects on the mantlepiece in *Journeys from Berlin/1971*.

production still
MURDER and murder
Kathleen Chalfant, Joanna Merlin,
Yvonne Rainer
photo: Esther Levine

Part of that difference has to do with the extraordinary force of the photographic, the archive of personal and public images that comprise our sense of our own history, and our broader relation to historicity as such. This force of the photographic, postmodernism has shown, comes from its own split, its negative and its developed print. On the one hand, photographs feed our deep longing for a transparent document, a record of the "real" event, while on the other, photographs continually flaunt their crops, their edits, their embroidered response to the "real" event. Perhaps this second aspect of the photographic could profitably be seen in relation to the strategies of the baroque. The first aspect, the transparent record, has a particular relevance to the work of Judson, and to Rainer's initial interest in the neutral-doer and tasklike movement performances.

After Rainer moved away from dance, she critiqued her search for the neutral doer, saying that it is impossible to repress entirely the self-expression in an act as apparently "neutral" as walking. Citing the work of Steve Paxton, Rainer realized that the embodied self, full of contradictions, moments of lucidity, and the ongoing drama of confusion, expresses itself by becoming a character, by entering a mode of performance that is both self-expressive and self-concealing. This is the contemporary version of the theatrum mundi. The illusion of neutrality must give way to a more radical fluid field in which operations of ideology and power can be exposed rather than disguised. This task is at once structural and individual. It is at once personal and public. It continues to clamor, despite all attempts to prune and repress its urgency now.

e-mail correspondence between sabine folie and peggy phelan

After Many a Summer Dies the Swan
Brooklyn Academy of Music 2000
White Oak Dance Project: Emily Coates
supported by Emmanuèle Phuon, Michael
Lomeka, Rosalynde LeBlanc, Mikhail
Baryshnikov, Raquel Aedo
photo: Stephanie Berger

after many a summer dies the swan: hybrid

videographers
Charles Atlas
Natsuko Inue

editors
Yvonne Rainer
Amanda Ault

choreography
Yvonne Rainer

from *After Many a Summer Dies the Swan*
commissioned by
The Baryshnikov Dance Foundation, 2000
performed by
The White Oak Dance Project
Raquel Aedo
Mikhail Baryshnikov
Emily Coates
Rosalynde LeBlanc
Michael Lomeka
Emmanuèle Phuon

literary and photographic sources
Carl Schorske, *Fin-de-Siècle Vienna:*
Politics and Culture
Allan Janik and Stephen Toulmin,
Wittgenstein's Vienna
Robert Musil, *The Man Without Qualities,* Vol. 1

music
Arnold Schoenberg, "Verklärte Nacht"
(Transfigured Night) performed by the Ensemble
InterContemporain conducted by Pierre Boulez

Support provided by the Wexner Center
Media Arts Program of Ohio State University
and by a grant from the Philadelphia Exhibitions
Initiative a program funded by The
Pew Charitable Trusts and administered by
The University of the Arts, Philadelphia

Sit-Around® Ball Chair concept and design
by June Ekman and Laurence Wilson

Thanks to Sabine Folie and Gudrun Ratzinger
the Kunsthalle Wien and the Osterreichische
Nationalbibliothek

Special thanks to Martha Gever

The printed texts contained in this installation have been gleaned, excerpted,
paraphrased, quoted, and appropriated primarily from the following three sources:

Carl Schorske's *Fin-de-Siècle Vienna: Politics and Culture*
Robert Musil's *The Man Without Qualities,* Vol. 1
Allan Janik's and Stephen Toulmin's *Wittgenstein's Vienna*

The passages printed in red are quotations or ideas of Oscar Kokoschka, Adolf Loos,
Arnold Schoenberg, and Ludwig Wittgenstein, four of the most radical innovators in
painting, architecture, music, and philosophy to emerge from *fin-de-siécle* Vienna.

These excerpts are the outcome of a fascinated inquiry that had its origin in my own
practice, but also in the courses in avant-garde film, video, and performance I have
been teaching intermittently for a number of years. Having early on acknowledged my
debt to the Futurist, Dadaist, and Surrealist movements by way of John Cage and
Robert Rauschenberg, I have Jenny-come-lately to research in any depth the cultural
and political milieu of turn-of-the-19th-century Vienna. Although I have continued
to feel more affinity with post-WWII art movements, the histories of that earlier
avant-garde offer the prospect of understanding a period of art-making in all
its complex relations to a prolonged historical crisis, that of the declining Austro-
Hungarian Empire.

Under the presumption of god-given entitlement, the Emperor Francis Joseph
reigned for almost 70 years in vacuous chaos, relying on ceremony as a cover for his
own personal failings to cope with problems of nationalism, industrialization and
social change, or to govern a mélange of Germans, Ruthenes, Italians, Slovaks,
Rumanians, Czechs, Poles, Magyars, Slovenes, Croats, Transylvanian Saxons, and Serbs.
The muddled liberal middle classes, consisting mainly of Germans and German
Jews, colluded in upholding him and ignoring the rising tides of clashing and

disenfranchised voices. As their political power waned and wealth grew, this haute bourgeoisie turned increasingly to art and theater for social advancement and as a refuge from unpleasant political reality.

In early 2000 the Baryshnikov Dance Foundation commissioned from me a 35-minute dance for the White Oak Dance Project, which I called "After Many a Summer Dies the Swan" after Aldous Huxley's 1939 novel of the same name about Hollywood decadence. (I subsequently learned that the title is also a line from Tennyson's "Tithonus.") The dance contains, along with a variety of movement configurations, spoken lines derived from famous and unknown people's death-bed utterances. The final rehearsals for the dance were videotaped by Charles Atlas and Natsuko Inue. The idea for integrating some of this footage with the Vienna material came partly from the title, which both elegiacally and ironically evokes a passing of time and life, or, more to the point, aristocratic life. Thus the passage of Mikhail Baryshnikov himself is also implicated—from *danseur noble* roles in classical ballet to his current interests in postmodern dance.

Beyond the resonance of the title, however, the twenty-first-century dance footage (itself containing forty year-old instances of my twentieth-century choreography) can be read multifariously, and paradoxically, as both the beneficiary of a cultural and economic elite and as an extension of an avant-garde tradition that revels in attacking that elite and its illusions of order and permanency. Or, finally, each dance image can be taken simply as a graphic or mimetic correlation with its simultaneous text. In other words, the relation of dance to text, rather than being thematically or graphically fixed, is constantly shifting. The musical accompaniment, Schoenberg's "Verklärte Nacht" (Transfigured Night), written in 1899, determines the half-hour duration of the installation and, in its haunting, erotic romanticism, soon to be overturned by Schoenberg himself, foreshadowed the death of an era.

opposite:
Mat, a section of *The Mind is a Muscle*
Anderson Theater 1968
Becky Arnold, William Davis

video still
After Many a Summer Dies the Swan:
Hybrid
Rosalynde LeBlanc rehearses *Mat*

Some may say the avant-garde has long been over. Be that as it may, the idea of it continues to inspire and motivate many of us with its inducement—in the words of playwright/director Richard Foreman—to "resist the present."

Needless to say, those details in this video that suggest correspondences with our present moment are not coincidental.

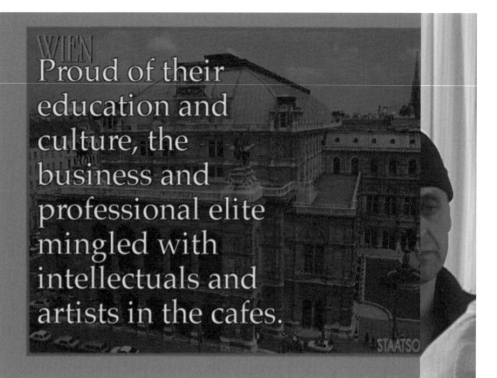

video still
*After Many a Summer Dies the Swan:
Hybrid*

To describe the use of aesthetic judgement or to describe what you mean by a cultured taste, you have to describe a culture.

The 19th century bequeathed to the 20th the power, arrogance, and brutality of certain massive structures.

Like all big cities it consisted of irregularity, change, sliding forward, not keeping in step, collisions of things and affairs, a seething vessel of buildings, laws, regulations, and historical traditions.

Proud of their education and culture, the business and professional elite mingled with intellectuals and artists in the cafes.

Emperor Francis Joseph pretended that change was not inevitable. The palace, with its oil lamps and 18th century sanitation, was preserved untouched.

The City of Dreams was to become, unknown to most, the "proving-ground of world destruction."

The Count, a progressive aristocratic patriot, recognized that the connection between the eternal verities and business was a matter of the greatest importance. For this reason he was not only a religious idealist but a passionate idealist in secular matters.

Every part of the female anatomy had to be concealed by clothing so cumbersome that it was impossible to dress oneself without assistance.

The Bank Manager did his duty sturdily as the great guiding ideals of tolerance, the dignity of man, free trade, disciplined conformity to the standards of good taste and action—reason and progress—were displaced by racial theories and street slogans.

The Emperor even instituted general manhood suffrage—against the will of the Liberals—as a last attempt to play off a new factor against all the unsatisfactory parties.

All that was good in the preceding period should not occur now.

Nobody knew exactly what was on the way; nobody was able to say whether it was to be a new art, a New Man, a new morality or perhaps a re-shuffling of society.

Meanwhile, they continued to have their initials embroidered on their undergarments.

Only a society which no longer desired to see things as they really are could possibly be so enamored of ornament.

And men of upright principles, confronted by helpless feelings of irrevocability, resorted to indignant denials or appeals to progress and superior reason.

Young girls were expected to be silly and untaught, well-educated and ignorant, curious and shy, and predisposed to be led and formed by a man in marriage. No wonder so many of Freud's patients were middle-aged bourgeois women.

The Count believed that everything would somehow turn out all right. He adhered to a mild realism of common sense, to a system of beautifully balanced compromises in every sphere.

Every time everyone was just beginning to rejoice in imperial absolutism, the Crown decreed that there must now again be a return to parliamentary government.

The struggles were so violent that they several times a year caused the machinery of State to jam and come to a dead stop. But in between everyone got on excellently with everyone else and behaved as though nothing had ever been the matter.

Failure above, explosion below.

Science and art replaced religion. Acquiring aesthetic culture was a substitute for entry into the historical aristocracy of pedigree.

The function of art is to shake us out of our complacency and comfort.

Ethics yielded its primacy to aesthetics, law to grace, knowledge of the world to the knowledge of one's feelings. A hedonistic self-perfection became the center of aspiration.

The pioneering Secession building used the form of a pagan temple to suggest the function of art as a surrogate religion for Vienna's secular intellectual elite.

Aristocratic decadence, parliamentary corruption, socialist class warfare, anarchist terror, anti-Semitic barbarism. They waited for these developments to disappear of their own accord.

A combination of mind, business, good living, and well-readness was everywhere while children worked 12 hours a day and slept under bridges.

Even at that time there were people who were prophesying the collapse of European civilization. It is significant that these people were all bad at mathematics at school.

It was said that during the last five years of the 19th century Austria-Hungary was a little world in which the big one was holding its try-outs for Europe's social and political disintegration.

For the Count it was quite clear that helping the poor was a knightly task and that for the true aristocracy there could be no great difference between a middle-class factory-owner and one of his workmen. "After all, we are all socialists at heart" was a pet saying of his.

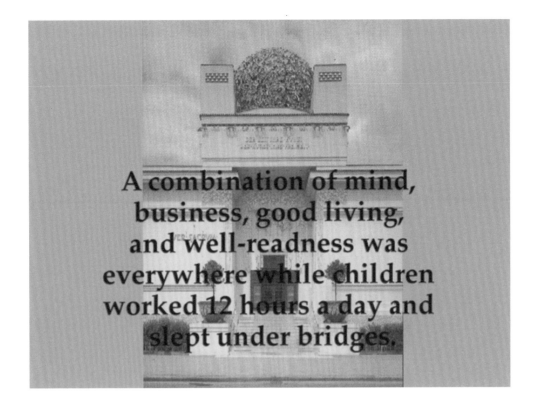

A combination of mind, business, good living, and well-readness was everywhere while children worked 12 hours a day and slept under bridges.

Plaques were erected in various villages showing the Emperor with his hand on the plow.

It was merely a world that had not been cleared away.

And one day one suddenly has a wild craving: Get out! Jump clear! It is a nostalgic yearning to be brought to a standstill, to cease evolving, to get stuck, to turn back to a point that lies before the wrong fork.

By the 1890s the heroes of the upper middle class were no longer political leaders, but actors, artists, and critics. The sphere of action of Viennese liberalism was constricted to the parquets of theaters on opening night.

In order to get clear about aesthetic words you have to describe ways of living.

The life of art became a substitute for the life of action.

For others, life was nasty, brutish, and short.

One can do nothing with contradictions except waste time puzzling over them.

If the common people could not be trusted, since they did not always understand, it was hoped that the spread of rational culture would one day lead to a broadly democratic order.

To the German petite bourgeoisie, the liberals were traitors to nationalism.

To the Marxists, the liberals' laissez faire, designed to break the arbitrary rule of privilege, was anathema.

To the peasant and artisan, liberalism meant capitalism and capitalism meant Jew.

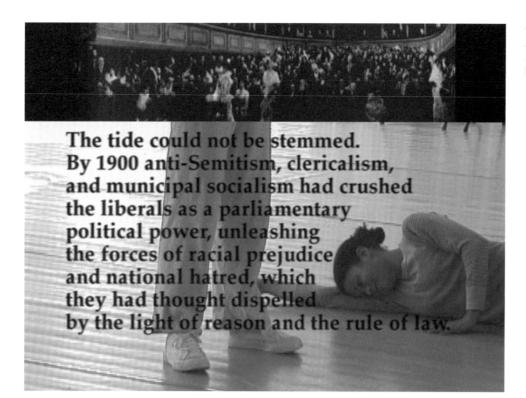

The tide could not be stemmed.
By 1900 anti-Semitism, clericalism,
and municipal socialism had crushed
the liberals as a parliamentary
political power, unleashing
the forces of racial prejudice
and national hatred, which
they had thought dispelled
by the light of reason and the rule of law.

Even the progressive Sigmund Freud, who in his youth had refused to doff his hat to the Emperor, celebrated the imperial veto of the popularly elected Karl Lueger for mayor. Lueger belonged to the anti-Semitic Christian Socialist party.

The tide could not be stemmed. By 1900 anti-Semitism, clericalism, and municipal socialism had crushed the liberals as a parliamentary political power, unleashing the forces of racial prejudice and national hatred, which they had thought dispelled by the light of reason and the rule of law.

Progress seemed at an end.

If it is art, it is not for all, and if it is for all, it is not art.

The century that had then just gone to its grave had not exactly distinguished itself in its second half. Nobody knew exactly what was on the way.

The world was all right as soon as they had regarded it. They showed a remarkable capacity for accepting catastrophes with stoical dignity.

Aestheticism, which elsewhere in Europe took the form of a protest against bourgeois civilization, became in Austria an expression of it.

The Permanent Secretary's wife's "at-homes" were a site of culture and capital, where the gentlemen and ladies of high society, by chatting with architects, politicians, and learned specialists on Boghaz Keui inscriptions, were also carrying out an important, though not precisely definable office.

Art means New Art.

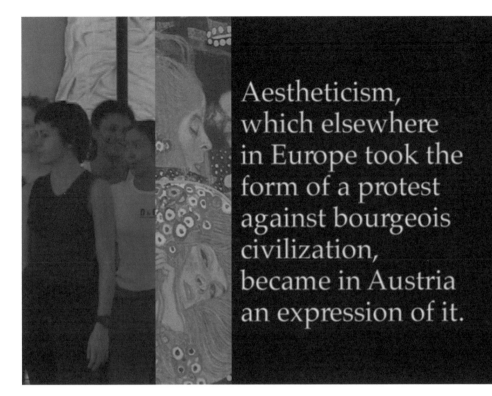

Aestheticism, which elsewhere in Europe took the form of a protest against bourgeois civilization, became in Austria an expression of it.

It was a natural conviction in her circle that one should not think too highly of anything to do with commerce, but like all people of bourgeois outlook she admired wealth in those depths of the heart that are quite independent of convictions.

All and sundry visited both the crystal palaces and the galleries of the avant-garde movements and those too of the avant-garde of the avant-garde … but all the relations between things had shifted slightly.

Modern art came into official favor just when modern parliamentary government was falling apart. The liberals thought they could outflank political tensions by a campaign of modernization.

Angry people—artisans cheated out of their past with no hope for future prospects, students dissatisfied with the pieties of the liberal-ethical tradition—formed the rootless social jetsam whom rightist leaders would later organize in the murky transition from democratic to protofascist politics.

Modern art would assuage the savage beasts.

The Permanent Secretary was a quiet habitué of bawdy houses and he transferred the regular rhythm of this custom into his marriage. The only things he took seriously were power, duty, high birth, and some way further down the scale, reason.

He opined that, although culture was the salt in the dish of life, yet the best society did not care for an over-salted cuisine.

In a healthier world use would be primary, and ornament would be criminal.

Her newest guest was not only rich but a man of notable intellect. He united the poles, usually separate in the world, of ideas and power. He preached nothing less than the union of soul and economics.

video still
*After Many a Summer Dies the Swan:
Hybrid*
Mikhail Baryshnikov performs
Valda's Solo while Michael Lomeka
executes backward somersaults
behind moving box

Themes of androgyny, homosexual reawakening, erotic liberation, and male fear of impotence all met with charges of indecency and immorality. The Ministry of Culture withdrew its support.

Everyone felt there must be a good deal that is true in what is said by someone who had known how to look after himself so well.

People liked listening to him because it was so nice that a man who had so many ideas also had money.

red fishling/fishling red
with a triple-bladed
knife I stab you dead
with my fingers rend you
in two
that there be an end
to this soundless circling.

The spirit of nationalism welling up all over Europe, with its surge of hostility to Jews, transformed respected liberals into members of a destructively analytical-minded alien race.

It was a remarkable time; you could move neither forward nor backward, and the present moment was quite unbearable.

As they adapted to the curbing of their political power, they embraced Klimt, Hofmannsthal, and Otto Wagner.

We must eliminate the reign of terror imposed on social life and art alike by the demands of style.

Klimt was initially heralded in the name of modernism, but his problematic, mysterious, and fantastic constructs violated the ideal of mastery of nature through science. The philistine press also found a way of identifying him with the Jews.

If I cannot bend the higher powers, I shall stir up hell.
(Freud quoting Virgil)

The Secession manifestoes called for cultural renewal and personal introspection, modern identity and asylum from modernity, truth and pleasure—contradictory possibilities compatible only in their common rejection of 19th century certainties.

Themes of androgyny, homosexual reawakening, erotic liberation, and male fear of impotence all met with charges of indecency and immorality. The Ministry of Culture withdrew its support.

If I cannot bend the higher powers, I shall stir up hell. (Freud quoting Virgil)

But the Secessionists now turned away from their unsettling findings to the more modest and profitable task of beautifying daily life and the domestic environment of the elite.

Their rebellion was incomplete.

Kokoschka shared with his older contemporaries—Hofmannsthal, Freud, Klimt, and Mach—a sense that the firm traditional coordinates of ordered time and space were losing their reliability, that the boundary between ego and world is permeable.

There was a general degeneration in the use of language. If the Emperor ruled by divine right, the question whether his political decisions were correct or mistaken was meaningless.

Wittgenstein's life-long efforts to separate language from value and representation from ethics may well date from his early life midst the corruptions of the Austro-Hungarian Empire.

In a culture overloaded with tawdry rubbish and meaningless etiquette, the rebellious young men rejected facial hair along with all other bourgeois superfluities.

video still
After Many a Summer Dies the Swan:
Hybrid
Emmanuèle Phuon, Michael Lomeka

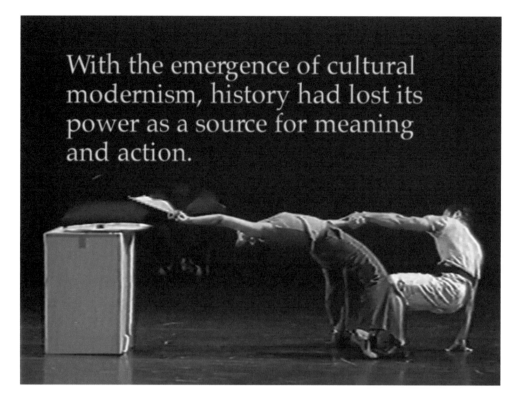

With the emergence of cultural modernism, history had lost its power as a source for meaning and action.

Tonality in music, the science of perspective, the Baroque status system in society, legal absolutism in politics – all were challenged by dissolution of tonality and hierarchical structure, erasure of ornament, ambiguity of direction, liberation of dissonance, psychological chaos, erosion of the fixed key, uncertainty of meaning… and WWI.

As soon as people learn to see what we are doing, then it will become impossible to commit mass crimes.

We must stop the penetration of life with art.

The time will come when the furnishings of a prison cell in the art nouveau style will be considered aggravation of the sentence.

Whatever serves a purpose must be excluded from the realm of art.

They rejected the use of art as a cultural cosmetic to screen the nature of reality.

But what are the human rights of those who still believe in defeated art, in defeated ideas?

With the emergence of cultural modernism, history had lost its power as a source for meaning and action.

Emmanuèle Phuon speaks:
In 1980 U.S. executives made 43 times more than factory workers.
In 1988 U.S. executives made 419 times more than factory workers.

Redeem us from our isolation!

video still
After Many a Summer Dies the Swan:
Hybrid
Emmanuèle Phuon, John Schuler
with section of Oskar Kokoschka's
"The Dreaming Boys"

**Yvonne Rainer 72 Franklin St. New York NY 10013 Tel/Fax: (212) 925-8809
email: whyrain@aol.com**

March 29, 2002

Professor Carl Schorske
Princeton University
Princton, N.J.

Dear Professor Schorske:

I am a friend and colleague of Hal Foster (at the Independent Study Program of
the Whitney Museum). Having just completed a half-hour videotape that is
heavily indebted to your research and writing, I thought you and Hal would be
interested in viewing it. Hal has offered to deliver this copy to you after he
himself has viewed the tape.

I have been working in the arts, mainly in New York, since 1960, in the areas of
choreography and film. Coming of age in the shadow of Merce Cunningham,
John Cage, Robert Rauschenberg, Maya Deren, and other cultural figures
prominent in the 50s and 60s, I have always considered myself a product of the
avant-garde, however diffused in meaning the term has become. So it was with
especial pleasure that I belatedly encountered your wonderful book with its
prescient resonances for my own era.

The tape will have a dual existence: As a projection that will move slowly along
the walls of a round room during an exhibition of my work that will open at the
Rosenwald-Wolf Gallery in Philadelphia on Oct. 19, 2002; and as an autonomous
videotape that will make the rounds mainly of university art departments.

I am enclosing a statement that will appear on a wall of the exhibition giving
historical and personal background information. If you would like a copyright
fee, please let me know .

In closing I must again reiterate my appreciation of and gratitude for your
brilliant work.

Very sincerely,

Yvonne Rainer

Yvonne Rainer

Princeton University

Department of History
129 Dickinson Hall
Princeton, New Jersey 08544-1017
Telephone: 609.258.4159
Fax: 609.258.5326

14 May, 2002

Dear Yvonne Rainer,

Thank you so much for sending me your fascinating "Dying Swan." On my first viewing, I could not bring the Texts (convincing though they were) into any relation to the dance. Only on the second go-around did I become aware that the screen-space and -time occupied by the dance was increasing to the finale, when it seemed to be delivering a big message with a strange mixture (very appropriate) of apodictic certainty and waffly group futility. It seemed to be saying with the body what not even Musil with all his Ulrich-ian rational penetration and

-2-

theatrical illusionism, could not convey more clearly .... It also did not at first make sense out of your choice of the "soft" early Schoenberg as the backdrop, when his later music that clearly resisted the present might have suited better the hard critical spirit of Loos, Musil and Wittgenstein .... Now I realize that the elegiac/erotic Verklärte Nacht conveyed ideally what was moving toward death. It was the Swan itself, around against which the analytic spirit grooved and which the muscular unsatisfied energies heaved. At the end, the dancers seemed to organize themselves to bear prophecy (with the outstretched finger); I shall not forget her.

I look forward to the Philadelphia showing of the video-along-the wall in October. Meanwhile, you have given me a lot to think about, and to re-consider. Many, many thanks.

Always yours,
Carl Schorske

P.S. Of course, no fee would be thinkable! It is an honor to have one's work so creatively used. -C.

rainer variations

A video constructed by Charles Atlas from material by and about Yvonne Rainer

video montage
Charles Atlas

videographers
Roddy Bogawa
Mary Patierno
Jason Simon

cinematographers
Robert Alexander (*Trio A*)
Michael Fajans (rehearsal)

sound recording
Harriet Hirshorn
Alisa Lebow

performers
Gregg Bordowitz
Kathleen Chalfant
Richard Move
Yvonne Rainer

source material
Yvonne Rainer
Gregg Bordowitz
Selected archives
The films of Yvonne Rainer

This project has been funded by a grant from the
Philadelphia Exhibitions Initiative, a program funded
by The Pew Charitable Trusts and administered
by The University of the Arts, Philadelphia.

In the spring of 2002 I handed over to Charles Atlas a collection of films and video-tapes in various formats that I had been accumulating with an eye to his editing them into what I call a "faux Rainer portrait" (though he may well call the final product something else).

The mix contained everything from interviews, rehearsals, films, and performance fragments to "impersonations," or actual Rainer interviews and rehearsals directed by me and re-enacted by others, in this case, the choreographer and Martha Graham impersonator Richard Move and noted actor Kathleen Chalfant.

I chose Charles Atlas for the task after seeing his chameleon video portrait of the British dancer/choreographer Michael Clark. The liberties that Atlas takes with the hallowed filmic and literary traditions of continuity and coherence appeal to my sense of mischief and play. —*Yvonne Rainer*

For me *Rainer Variations* is a hybrid: a weave of impressionistic portrait, found footage construction, and video sampler. Aside from formal issues, Yvonne Rainer's knotty process of thinking, her unique brand of humor, and her engaging presence are the things that were foremost in my mind as I worked on the tape. What I hope will emerge from this process is an interrogative portrait of an artist for whom I have great respect and affection. —*Charles Atlas*

1961

One Night Only
1961
Monday, July 31, at 8:40 p.m.

AN EVENING OF DANCE

PROGRAM:

1. LITTLE KOOTCH PIECE #2

    music, Richard Maxfield
    choreography, James Waring
    danced by Aileen Passloff, Fred Herko

2. THREE SATIE SPOONS

    music, Erik Satie
    choreographed and danced by Yvonne Rainer

3. POSSIBILITIES FOR A PLEASANT OUTING

    music, Fred Herko
    choreographed and danced by Fred Herko

4. ROSEFISH

    music, Terry Jennings
    costume, Remy Charlip
    choreographed and danced by Aileen Passloff

5. THE BELLS: A Study

    unaccompanied
    choreographed and danced by Yvonne Rainer

6. PRELUDE AND DANCE

    music, Joseph and Johan Strauss, jr.
    choreographed by John Herbert McDowell

THE LIVING THEATRE   Air-Conditioned
14th Street and Sixth Avenue CH 3-4569

All Tickets: $2.00

program
The Living Theater
1961

chronology

1934
Born November 24 in San Francisco to Joseph and Jeannette Rainer; father an Italian-born anarchist house painter/contractor; mother—born in Brooklyn to Jewish immigrants from Warsaw—a secretary until motherhood; brother, Ivan is almost four years older.

1943
Father takes her to see Carl Dreyer's *The Passion of Joan of Arc* at the Palace of the Legion of Honor.

1943–46
Mother takes her to ballet and opera: *Swan Lake, Carmen, La Bohème, La Traviata,* to name just a few.

1946
Sees Maxwell Anderson's *Winterset* at the Washington Street Playhouse with father and brother. They sit in the front row of an otherwise empty theater.

1950
Sees Roland Petit's dance company at the Curran Theater and Jean Cocteau's *Orphée* at the Larkin Theater; returns three times in the same week to see the latter.

1952
Graduates from Lowell High School.

1952 – 53
Attends San Francisco Junior College.

1953 – 54
Enrolls at UC Berkeley, drops out after one week; works in a factory operating a machine that stuffs coupons into envelopes; drives to Chicago with John Bottomley. There she works as a roller-skating order filler in a wholesale dry goods warehouse.

1954 – 55
Leaves Bottomley and returns to San Francisco; works in several offices as a figure clerk, while studying acting at the Washington Street Playhouse; is a regular at The Cellar to hear Lawrence Ferlinghetti, Kenneth Rexroth, Kenneth Patchen, and others read poetry to jazz accompaniment. Meets Al Held there.

1955 – 56
Begins living with Al Held; sees Allen Ginsberg read *Howl* at the Six Gallery. When Held leaves for New York, she follows.

1956 – 57
Works as artists' model and part-time typist; studies acting with Lee Grant at the Herbert Berghof Studio; visits galleries on East 10th Street; hangs out at the Cedar Bar with Held, George Sugarman, Ronald Bladen, Shirley Kaplan, and Doris Casella.

Studies modern dance with Edith Stephen; sees Merce Cunningham rehearsing in Stephen's studio; sees Erick Hawkins' *Here and Now with Watchers* at the 92nd Street Y and contemplates pursuing a dance career; studies Afro-Cuban dance with Emile Faustin.

1958
Studies "body work" with Allan Wayne, and Afro-Cuban dance with Syvilla Fort.

Sees Robert Rauschenberg's one-man show at the Castelli Gallery; sees *The Connection* at the Living Theater; sees Balanchine's *Agon* and Martha Graham in *Cave of the Heart*.

1959
Separates from Al Held.

Asks mother for economic support; takes three classes a day: two at the Graham School and one at Ballet Arts with various teachers – Nina Stroganova, Lisan Kay, Lynn Golding, et al.

Attends screenings of early cinema at the Museum of Modern Art; sees Merce Cunningham's *Antic Meet;* meets Nancy Meehan.

1960
Meets Simone Forti and Robert Morris.

At The Living Theater sees Maya Deren's *Meshes of the Afternoon* and *At Land*; Aileen Passlof's *Tea at the Palaz of Hoon*; and Bertolt Brecht's *In the Jungle of Cities.*

Sees Martha Graham's *Clytemnestra* on Broadway and Jean Genet's *The Blacks* at St. Mark's Playhouse.

yvonne rainer: radical juxtapositions 1961–2002   134

Works with Meehan and Forti in weekly improvisational sessions at Dance Players on 6th Avenue
(since torn down).

Attends Ann Halprin's summer workshop in
Kentfield, CA, along with Trisha Brown, Ruth
Emerson, June Ekman, A.A. Leath, and La Monte
Young, who teaches a sound course, during
which Yvonne Rainer makes *Sonata for Screen
Door, Flashlight,* and *Dancer.*

Begins eight-year study with Merce Cunningham;
shares a fifth-floor walk-up studio with Forti and
Morris; takes ballet classes with James Waring
and composition with Robert Dunn; attends
weekly events at Yoko Ono's loft on Chambers
Street.

Sees Jim Dine's *Car Crash* at the Reuben
Gallery; sees David Tudor perform John Cage's
4'33" at the 92nd Street Y.

Performs in Forti's *See Saw* at the Reuben
Gallery Christmas show, NYC, December 16.

1961
Sees Cunningham's *Aeon* and Stephen Tropp's
Poems for the Theater I and II.

Performs in Forti's *Evening of Dance
Constructions* in Ono's loft.

Performs *Three Satie Spoons* – a solo made
in Dunn's class—with another solo *The Bells,* at
The Living Theater, July 31.

Dances in the James Waring Dance Company.

Begins sharing a studio with Waring and Passlof.

Auditions *Three Satie Spoons* for a Young
Choreographers' concert at the 92nd Street Y
and is rejected.

1962
Shares an evening with Fred Herko; presents
Satie for Two (duet with Trisha Brown; music:
Erik Satie), *Three Seascapes* (solo; music: Sergei
Rachmaninoff and La Monte Young) and *Grass*
(duet with Dariusz Hochman; music: various).
Maidman Playhouse, NYC, March 5.

Dance for 3 People and 6 Arms (with Trisha
Brown, William Davis) at the Theater of the
Riverside Church, NYC, April.

Auditions for Al Carmines at Judson Church
(along with Ruth Emerson and Steve Paxton).

Ordinary Dance (solo, also presents *Dance
for 3 People and 6 Arms*); sees David Gordon's
Mannequin Dance and Steve Paxton's *Transit*
and performs in the latter's *Proxy,* all on the
same program.
First Concert of Dance, Judson Church, NYC,
July 6.

Three solos and *Dance Lecture,* KQED-TV,
San Francisco, August.

Attends weekly sessions of dance workshop in
the Judson Church gym.

Performs *From the Solo Section* (from *Terrain*)
Beverly Blossom's Studio, NYC, December 1.

Satie for Two
studio photo 1962
Yvonne Rainer,
Trisha Brown
costumes by
James Waring

below:
poster
Maidman Playhouse
1962
designed by Ray
Johnson

THE COMPANIES INCLUDE:
JAMES WARING,
NICOLA CERNOVICH,
DARIUS HOCKMAN,
RAY JOHNSON,
ALAN MARLOWE,
VALDA SETTERFIELD,
DICK HIGGINS, JR.,
MISS RAINER
AND
MR. HERKO
WILL OFFER A WORK FOR
DANCERS & ACTORS,
EDGE
MUSIC JOHN COLTRANE,
PAMELA DAVIES, PETER HARTMAN,
DAVID WALKER
COSTUMES JAMES WARING

FURTHER INFORMATION WRITE
NEW YORK POETS THEATRE
309 EAST HOUSTON ST, NYC 2,NY

THE NEW YORK POETS THEATRE
PRESENTS AN EVENING OF DANCE

BY ✳ YVONNE RAINER AND
● ✳ FRED HERKO WORKS

8:40 P.M. MONDAY, MARCH 5TH, AT THE
MAIDMAN PLAYHOUSE, 416 W. 42 ST.
ADMISSION $2.00 RESERVATIONS OR 7-9150

poster
Wexner Center
for the Arts 1995
The Ohio State
University
original photos:
Peter Moore
(George Segal's
farm 1963)

1963
We Shall Run (12 performers, music: Berlioz's
Requiem), *Three Seascapes,* and *Word Words*
(collaboration with Steve Paxton).
Judson Church, NYC, January 29.

Shares a concert with William Davis, Phyllis
Lamhut, Albert Reid: presents *Duet Section*
(from *Terrain,* with Trisha Brown; music: Philip
Corner) and *Ordinary Dance.*
Judson Hall (now CAMI), NYC, February 15.

Terrain (evening-length work performed by
Trisha Brown, William Davis, Judith Dunn, Steve
Paxton, Albert Reid; music: Philip Corner and
Johann Sebastian Bach; lighting: Robert
Rauschenberg).
Judson Church, NYC, April 28; later presented
in the *Concert of Dance #5* produced by the
Washington Gallery of Modern Art at America
on Wheels, Washington, D.C., May 9.

Improvisation on the Roof of a Chicken Coop
(collaboration with Trisha Brown).
George Segal's farm, North Brunswick, NJ,
May 19.

Person Dance, from *Dance for Fat Man,
Dancer,* and *Person* (solo, later called S*ome
Thoughts on Improvisation*).
The Pocket Follies, Pocket Theater, NYC, June 10.

Performs in the work of Steve Paxton, Lucinda
Childs, Carolee Schneemann, Philip Corner.

Performs in Gertrude Stein's *What Happened*
(directed by Al Carmines and Lawrence
Kornfield).
Judson Church, NYC, October 4.

Room Service (for 12 performers, collaboration
with Charles Ross) and *Shorter End of a Small
Piece* (group).
Judson Church, NYC, November 10 – 12.

1964
Begins living with Robert Morris.

Performs in the work of Aileen Passlof, Judith
Dunn; studies ballet with Mia Slavenska.

Makes *At My Body's House* (solo, wireless
sound transmission by Billy Klüver; music:
Dietrich Buxtehude).
State University College, New Paltz, NY,
January 30.

Dialogues (with Lucinda Childs, Judith Dunn,
Deborah Hay, Alex Hay, Tony Holder, Steve
Paxton).
Surplus Dance Theater, Stage 73, NYC,
February 9 (series includes revival of *Three
Seascapes*).

Some Thoughts on Improvisation (solo).
Once Festival, Ann Arbor, MI, Feb. 27; also in
Events and Entertainments, Pocket Theater,
NYC, March 16.

Part of a Sextet (duet with Robert Morris).
Judson Church, NYC, June 20.

Incidents (duet with Larry Loonin).
Cafe Cino, NYC, July.

Improvisation (with Jill Johnston).
Washington Square Gallery, NYC, July 31.

Travels to Stockholm with Morris to perform in Music and Dance Festival with Cage, Cunningham, Rauschenberg, Paxton and Deborah and Alex Hay; presents *At My Body's House, Part of a Sextet,* and *Some Thoughts on Improvisation.*
Moderna Museet, Stockholm, Sweden, August.

Accompanies Morris to Düsseldorf where he prepares a one-man show; meets Josef Beuys, who stage-manages a dance concert she and Morris share (same program as above plus *Part of a Sextet No. 2,* or *Rope Duet*).
Düsseldorf Kunstakademie, Düsseldorf, Germany, October 24.

Three Seascapes
Stage 73 1964
original
choreography 1962
photo: Peter Moore
© Estate of P.
Moore/VAGA, NYC

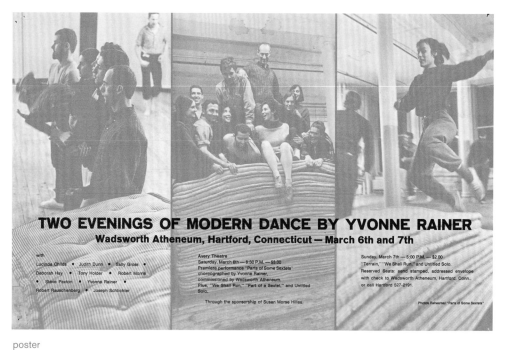

poster
Wadsworth
Atheneum 1965

1965
Parts of Some Sextets (program also includes
We Shall Run and *New Untitled Solo with Pink
T-Shirt, Blue Bloomers, Red Ball,* and *Bach's
Toccata and Fugue in D Minor* [later referred to
as *Untitled Solo with Bach's etc*]).
Wadsworth Atheneum, Hartford, CT, March 6.

Performs in Robert Morris's *Check* and
Waterman Switch (program includes *Untitled
Solo* and *Parts of Some Sextets*).
Judson Church, NYC, March 23 – 25.

Performs in Dick Higgin's opera, *Hrusalk*
(wearing a lead brassiere constructed by
Robert Morris).
Café à GoGo, NYC, Winter.

Revival of *Room Service*.
First New York Theater Rally, NYC,
May 11 – 13.

Performs in Beverly Blossom's dance concert.
92nd Street Y, April.

Revival of *Three Satie Spoons*.
Festival of the Avant-garde, Judson Hall (now
CAMI), NYC, August 26.

program
Wadsworth
Atheneum 1965

right:
poster
Judson Church
1966
designed
by David Gordon

Solo Concert.
Commonwealth Institute, London, September 13.

Scandinavian tour (shared with Robert Morris), Stockholm, Malmo, Copenhagen, September.

1966
Sees Warhol's *Chelsea Girls* and *Henry Geldzahler* at the New Yorker Theater, NYC.

The Mind is a Muscle, Part I (*Trio A* with Steve Paxton and David Gordon), *Rope Duet* (from *Parts of Some Sextets,* with Alfred Kurchin), and *Partially Improvised Solo with Bach's Toccata and Fugue in D Minor* on a program shared with Paxton and Gordon.
Judson Memorial Church, NYC, January 10 – 12.

Performs in "An Evening of Dancing and Talking" with David Gordon, Jill Johnston.
Fairleigh Dickinson University, NJ, February 25.

The Mind is a Muscle (40-minute version with Becky Arnold, William Davis, Barbara Dilley, David Gordon, and Peter Saul).
Now Festival, Washington, D.C., April 29; Judson Church, NYC, May 22 – 24.

Carriage Discreteness (12 performers, on an evening shared with John Cage).
Festival of Theater and Engineering, 69th Regiment Armory, NYC, October 15.

Becomes gravely ill; asks William Davis to make an 8mm film of her moving fingers (*Hand Movie*) while she is in the hospital.

1967
Sees Michael Snow's *Wavelength* at Anthology Film Archives, NYC.

Convalescent Dance (*Trio A* as a solo).
Angry Arts Week, Hunter Playhouse, NYC, February 2.

The Mind is a Muscle, (abridged version with William Davis).
Festival of Two Worlds, Spoleto, Italy, July.

Mat (from *The Mind is a Muscle* performed by Becky Arnold & William Davis with a voice-over reading of a letter from Yvonne Rainer's surgeon).

"Inside Modern Dance."
Choreoconcerts, The New School, NYC, October 24.

Volleyball (16mm film, shot by Bud Wirtschafter)

Featured in "One Hundred American Women of Accomplishment," *Harper's Bazaar*. Rainer is no. 100; Lady Byrd Johnson is no. 1.

1968
Untitled Work for 40 People.
New York University Dance Dept., NYC, February

The Mind is a Muscle (evening-length, with Becky Arnold, Gay DeLanghe, Barbara Dilly, David Gordon, Steve Paxton, Harry De Dio).
Brandeis University, Waltham, MA, January 12; Anderson Theater, NYC, April 11, 14, 15.

Sees Steve Paxton's *Satisfyin' Lover.*

original manuscript for "A Quasi Survey of Some 'Minimalist' Tendencies in the Quantitatively Minimal Dance Activity Midst the Plethora, or an Analysis of *Trio A*," published in *Minimal Art, A Critical Anthology*, Gregory Battcock, ed., New York: E. P. Dutton, 1968

Convalescent Dance (*Trio A* as a solo)
Hunter Playhouse 1967
photo: Peter Moore
© Estate of P. Moore/VAGA, NYC

Performance Demonstration no. 1 (large group). Library and Museum of the Performing Arts, NYC, September 16.

Body and Snot (solo) "Inside Modern Dance" II. Choreoconcerts, The New School, NYC, October 8.

Trio Film (Phill Niblock films Steve Paxton and Becky Arnold nude in Virginia Dwan's apartment in the Dakota, 16mm).

Two Trios (*Trio Film* simultaneously projected with section from *Rose Fractions*, performed by Yvonne Rainer, Becky Arnold, Barbara Dilley). Theater of the Riverside Church, NYC, October 18.

Northeast Passing (for 30 students) during a one-month residency at Goddard College, Plainfield, VT. While there she asks Roy Levin to film the interior of a chicken coop (*Rhode Island Red,* 16mm).

1969
Receives first grant, a Guggenheim Fellowship ($9,500).

*Rose Fractions (*evening-length, large group; music: Chambers Brothers).
Festival of Modern Dance, Billy Rose Theater, NYC, February 6, 8.

Performance Fractions for the West Coast (large group)

Grand Union Dreams
Emmanuel Midtown YM-YWHA 1971
Trisha Brown on ball, Fernando Torm in box
photo: Susan Horwitz

Vancouver Art Gallery, April 2 (beginning of West Coast tour shared with Glenn Lewis); Old Los Angeles Music Conservatory, April 14; Mills College, Oakland, CA, April 25.

Continuous Project – Altered Daily (with Becky Arnold, Barbara Dilley, Douglas Dunn, David Gordon, Steve Paxton).
University of Illinois at Urbana-Champaign, IL, May 8, also part of *Connecticut Composite* (evening-length, including *CP-AD,* 60 performers, music: Ike & Tina Turner); Connecticut College, New London, CT, July 19

Line (16mm film, shot by Phill Niblock).

1970
CP-AD (with Becky Arnold, Barbara Dilley, Douglas Dunn, David Gordon, Steve Paxton; music: Ike & Tina Turner, George Harrison). Whitney Museum of American Art, NYC, March 31 – April 2.

M-Walk (from *The Mind is a Muscle,* large group), a street action protesting U.S. invasion of Cambodia.
Greene St., NYC, May.

Separates from Robert Morris.

Begins performing with The Grand Union.

CP-AD and *WAR* (large group) .
Douglass College, New Brunswick, NJ, November 6; Smithsonian Institute, November 19; Loeb Student Center, New York University, NYC, November 22.

Trio A with Flags (performed by Barbara Dilley, David Gordon, Nancy Green, Steve Paxton, Yvonne Rainer, Lincoln Scott).
People's Flag Show, Judson Church, NYC, November 9.

1971
Travels in India for six weeks on an E.A.T. (Experiments in Art and Technology) fellowship.

Performs in David Gordon's *Sleepwalking.*
Emmanuel Midtown YM-YWHA, NYC, May 15.

Grand Union Dreams, (evening-length, large group).
Emmanuel Midtown YM-YWHA, NYC, May 16.

Numerous Frames (50 performers).
Walker Art Center, Minneapolis, MN, May 29.

Receives first grant from the National Endowment for the Arts ($9,750).

1972
In residence at Oberlin College with The Grand Union, makes *In the College* (large group) on a program shared with David Gordon. Oberlin College, Ohio, January 21.

Sees Hollis Frampton's film, *Poetic Justice.*

Inner Appearances (solo with vacuum cleaner) and *Valda's Solo* (from *Performance,* performed by Valda Setterfield).
"Dancing Ladies" (a series organized by James Waring. Yvonne Rainer takes umbrage at the title of concert).
Theater for the New City, NYC, March 23 – 27.

"PERFORMANCE"

1. Inner Appearances (1972) (Final slide J / tape #1 dreams) "Cliché"
   premiere F   John-slides John-slides

2. address audience - ask for Fernando volunteer "with
   modest deportment & good will."

2. Grand Union Dreams - photos & script Y, Sh, V, "F" John-slides

3. Valdes solo   (Y gives "F" instructions over PA offstage
                                    re: Story, box, Drama, Sun

4. Story   YJS   "F" reads   S YJS   (Valda in box)

5. Box, Walk, Light Changes   V, S, Y - "F" in box   tape #1
                                    John, Yvonne, left, run

6. Film (John)   (Stones) tape #2
                            (people lie on backs)

7. Lulu (follow-spot → John SYVJ (Hofstra person on f-spot)

8. Drama (" " → John   tape #2 (Shirley + John
                                    reading script)

9. Sun

9. Sun
10. 3 Satie Spoons (1961)   "F" reads
                            Phil Corner piano
                            (Shirley's Dream) - tape #2

[END]
Dreams of our time - { Oberlin College students
                     { David Gordon and
                     { Shirley Soffer

"No Expectations" Rolling Stones } from "In the College"
Story   } Oberlin College 1972
Film   } Jan.
Lulu

I am grateful to Babette Mangolte for her photographic
assistance. YR

technician   John Erdman
protagonists Valda Setterfield, Shirley Soffer, Fernando Torm
director   Yvonne Rainer   "in absentia"

Meets Babette Mangolte and begins to talk
about shooting a feature film.

Performance (evening-length, with John Erdman,
Valda Setterfield, Shirley Soffer, Epp Kotkas,
James Barth, Fernando Torm).
Hofstra University, Hempstead, NY, March 21;
Whitney Museum of American Art, April 21;
Festival of Music and Dance (selections
performed by Yvonne Rainer and Philip Glass).
L'Attico, Rome, June 14.

Lives of Performers
Cinematographer: Babette Mangolte.

This is the story of a woman who...
(evening-length, performed with John Erdman).
Festival D'Automne à Paris, Musée d'Art
Moderne de la Ville, Paris, November 15.

Stops working with The Grand Union.

1973
This is the story of a woman who...
(with John Erdman, Shirley Soffer;
lighting: Jennifer Tipton; film and slides:
Babette Mangolte).
Theater for the New City, NYC, March 16.

1974
Begins teaching at the Independent Study
Program of the Whitney Museum of
American Art.

program
and poster
Hofstra University
1972

Film About a Woman Who...
Cinematographer: Babette Mangolte.

Kristina (for a ... Novella) (evening-length, with John Erdman)
S.U.N.Y., Purchase, NY, October 11;
Walker Art Center, Minneapolis, MN,
May 17, 18, 1975.

1975
Receives first grant from the New York State
Council on the Arts ($5,000).

Performs in Babette Mangolte's film, *What Maizie Knew.*

Revival of *Trio A* (performed by Sara Rudner).
Movement Research, Ethnic Folk Arts Center,
NYC, April 23.

Works with Babette Mangolte in New York
and Benjamin Buchloh in Cologne on "Kristina
(For a ... Opera)" a photo-romanza published
in the journal, *Interfunctionen.*

1976
Kristina Talking Pictures
Cinematographers: Babette Mangolte,
Roger Dean.

1976 – 77
Receives a Deutscher Akademischer
Austauschdienst (DAAD) and spends a year in
West Berlin, where she conceives a film about
political violence.

Performs in Ulrike Ottinger's film, *Madame X,*
on Lake Constance.

1978
Revival of *Trio A* (performed by Yvonne Rainer
for 16mm film produced by Sally Banes).
Cinematographer: Robert Alexander.

1980
Journeys from Berlin/1971
Cinematographer: Carl Teitelbaum.

1981
Journeys From Berlin/1971 wins Special
Achievement Award from the Los Angeles Film
Critics' Association.

1982
Revival of *Trio A* (performed by Yvonne Rainer)
Judson Dance Project.
St. Mark's Church, NYC, June.

1983
Sees Trisha Brown's *Set and Reset.*

1984
Meets Martha Gever.

1985
The Man Who Envied Women
Cinematographer: Mark Daniels.

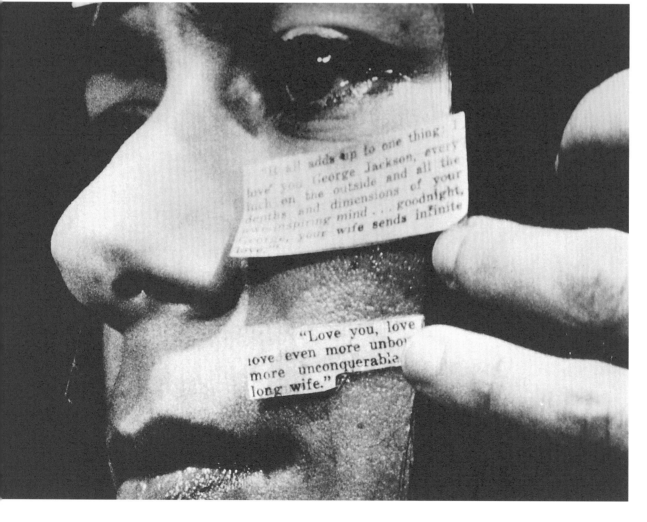

frame enlargement
*Film About
a Woman Who...*
(1974)

1988
Receives Maya Deren Award (American Film Institute).

Receives a Rockefeller Fellowship and second Guggenheim Fellowship.

1989
The Man Who Envied Women is screened on *Independent Focus*, WNET-TV, August 13.

1990
Privilege
Cinematographer: Mark Daniels.

Receives James D. Phelan Award in Filmmaking.

Receives MacArthur Fellowship.

Begins living with Martha Gever.

1991
Privilege wins the Filmmakers' Trophy at the Sundance Film Festival, Park City, Utah and the Geyer Werke Prize at the Munich Documentary Film Festival.

1992
Revival of *Mat* (from *The Mind is a Muscle*, performed by Sally Silvers) Movement Research. Judson Church, NYC, June 19.

Revival of *Trio A* (performed by Clarinda MacLow).
Serious Fun Festival, New York State Theater, Lincoln Center, NYC, July 29.

Privilege is screened on *Independent Focus*, WNET-TV, November 8.

1995
Receives a Wexner Prize.

1996
Revivals of *Trio A* (performed by Jean Guizerix) and *Continuous Project–Altered Daily* (reconstructed fragments performed by the Quatuor Albrecht Knust).
Montpellier Dance Festival, Montpellier, France, June 25.

MURDER and murder
Cinematographer: Stephen Kazmierski.

1997
MURDER and murder wins the Teddy Award for Best Essay Film at the Berlin Film Festival.

Revivals of *Trio A* (performed by Yvonne Rainer & Clarinda MacLow) and *CP-AD* (performed by Quatuor Albrecht Knust) and *Three Satie Spoons* (performed by Sally Silvers).
Talking Dancing Conference, Stockholm, Sweden, August.

1999
MURDER and murder wins the Special Jury Award at the Miami Lesbian and Gay Film Festival.

Revival of *Trio A with Flags* (12 performers) "No Limits: a Celebration of Freedom and Art" Judson Memorial Church, NYC, April 22, 23.

frame enlargement
MURDER and murder (1996)
Joanna Merlin,
Kathleen Chalfant

Trio A Pressured (performed by Colin Beatty, Pat Catterson, Douglas Dunn, Steve Paxton, and Yvonne Rainer).
Movement Research, Judson Church, NYC, Ocober 4.

Mikhail Baryshnikov invites her to make a dance for his White Oak Dance Project. She nearly pees in her pants.

2000
Richard Move invites her to participate in his *Martha @ Mother* variety show. They collaborate on *Debate 2000. Valda's Solo* (from *Performance*) is performed by Mikhail Baryshnikov as part of the show. Mother, NYC, May 3 – 5.

After Many a Summer Dies the Swan (30 minutes, commissioned by the Baryshnikov Dance Foundation, with Raquel Aedo, Mikhail Baryshnikov, Emily Coates, Rosalynde LeBlanc, Michael Lomeka, Emmanuèle Phuon).
Brooklyn Academy of Music, Brooklyn, NY, June 7, 9, 10.

*After Many
a Summer Dies
the Swan*
Brooklyn Academy
of Music 2000
Emmanuèle Phuon,
Rosalynde
LeBlanc, Michael
Lomeka (with
pillow on head),
Mikhail Baryshnikov
photo:
Stephanie Berger

Receives NY Dance and Performance Award
("Bessie").

Meetings (improvisation with Xavier Le Roy).
Berlin International Dance Festival, August 23, 26.

Sees Steve Paxton's *Ash*.

2001
Revival of *Talking Solo* (from *After Many a
Summer Dies the Swan,* performed by Michael
Lomeka).
Talking Dance Festival, The Kitchen, NYC,
January 31 – February 3.

Revivals of *Chair/Pillow* (from *Continuous
Project – Altered Daily*), *Trio A Pressured,*
and *Talking Solo* (performed by the White Oak
Dance Project).
PAST/forward, Brooklyn Academy of Music,
Brooklyn, NY, June 5 – 9.

Inner Appearances (slide and prop Installation)
and *Trio A* (video projection).
"A Baroque Party," Kunsthalle, Vienna, Austria,
June 12 – September 16.

Sees Trisha Brown's *Luci Mie Traditrici*.

Revival of *CP-AD* (performed by the Quatuor
Albrecht Knust).
Festival Nouvelle Danse de Montréal, Montreal,
Canada, September 25, 26.

Performs in revival of Philip Corner's *Certain
Distilling Processes.*
Greenwich House, NYC, December 2.

2002
Debate 2002, performed by Richard Move and
Yvonne Rainer as part of Move's *Martha at the
Pillow,* also includes revival of *Three Seascapes*
(performed by Patricia Hoffbauer).
Jacob's Pillow, Beckett, MA, August 8 –11.

Revival of *Three Seascapes* (performed by
Patricia Hoffbauer).
Movement Research/Judson Church, NYC,
September 30.

Asks Charles Atlas to edit a "faux Rainer video
portrait" from material supplied by her (*Rainer
Variations*).

After Many a Summer Dies the Swan: Hybrid
(video installation); *Rainer Variations* (video
construction by Charles Atlas from material by
and about Yvonne Rainer); *Inner Appearances*
(slide and prop installation) in a solo exhibition:
*Yvonne Rainer: Radical Juxtapositions
1961 – 2002.*
Rosenwald–Wolf Gallery, The University of the
Arts, Philadelphia, October 19 – November 30.

Revival of *Trio A Pressured* (performed by the
White Oak Dance Project).
European tour, Fall.

filmography / videography

1966   *Hand Movie*
        8mm, b/w, 5 min.

1967   *Volleyball*
        16mm, b/w, 10 min.

1968   *Rhode Island Red*
        16mm, b/w, 10 min.
        (never publicly screened)

        Trio Film
        16mm, b/w, 13 min.

1969   *Line*
        16mm, b/w, 10 min.

1972   *Lives of Performers*
        16mm, b/w, 90 min.

1974   *Film About a Woman Who...*
        16mm, b/w & color, 105 min.

1976   *Kristina Talking Pictures*
        16mm, color & b/w, 90 min.

1978   *Trio A*
        16mm, b/w, 10 min.

1980   *Journeys from Berlin/1971*
        16mm, color, 125 min.

1985   *The Man Who Envied Women*
        16mm, color & b/w, 125 min.

1990   *Privilege*
        16mm, color & b/w, 100 min.

1996   *MURDER and murder*
        16mm, color, 113 min.

2002   *After Many a Summer Dies the Swan:*
        Hybrid
        video, 30 min.

In the U.S. the 16mm feature films listed above
are distributed by Zeitgeist Films, 247 Centre St.,
New York, N.Y. 10013 (tel.: 212 274-1989;
fax: 212 274-1644). The short films are distributed
by Yvonne Rainer, 72 Franklin Street, New York,
NY 10013 (whyrain@aol.com). The video is distributed
by Video Data Bank, The School of the Art Institute
of Chicago, 112 South Michigan Ave., Chicago,
IL 60603 (tel: 312 345-3550; fax: 312 541-8073).
Trio A is distributed by John Mueller, Dance
Film Archive, Mershon Center, 1501 Neil Ave., Ohio
State University, Columbus, Ohio 43201-2602
(fax: 614 292-2407; bbbb@osu.edu).

selected major screenings

1968
Hand Movie
Cinematographer: William Davis
Volleyball
Cinematographer: Bud Wirtschafter

Anderson Theater, NYC, April 11 (premiered
    with *The Mind is a Muscle*).

Trio Film
Cinematographer: Phill Niblock
performers: Becky Arnold, Steve Paxton

Theater of the Riverside Church, NYC, October
    18 (premiered in *Two Trios*).
Billy Rose Theater, NYC, February 6, 8, 1969
    (screened in *Rose Fractions*).

1969
Line
Cinematographer: Phill Niblock
performer: Susan Marshal

"Coulisse," program of artists' films at Paula
    Cooper Gallery, NYC, June 13.
Festival of Music and Dance, L'Attico, Rome,
    June 17 (screened in program of Rainer's
    short films with Steve Paxton simultaneously
    performing *Trio A* for one hour).

1972
Lives of Performers
Cinematographer: Babette Mangolte

"New Forms in Film," Guggenheim Museum,
    NYC, August 12.
Festival of Music and Dance, L'Attico, Rome.
Festival D'Automne à Paris, Paris, September.
Women's Film Festival, Whitney Museum of
    American Art, NYC, 1973.
Festival of Avant-Garde Film, London, 1973.
Elgin Theater, NYC, 1973.
Millennium, NYC, 1973.
Vanguard Theater, Los Angeles, 1974.

Walker Art Center, Minneapolis, MN, 1974.
New Forms in Film, Montreux, Switzerland, 1974.
Cannes Film Festival, 1974.
Films by and about Women, Paris, 1974.
Mannheim Film Festival, Mannheim, Germany, 1974.
Edinburgh Film Festival, Edinburgh, Scotland, 1975.
Film as Vision, Film at the Public, NYC, 1988.

1974
Film About a Woman Who...
Cinematographer: Babette Mangolte

"Recent American Art," National Gallery of
    Victoria, Melbourne, Australia.
Projekt '74, Cologne, Germany.
Carnegie Institute, Pittsburgh.
New American Filmmakers Series, Whitney
    Museum of American Art, NYC.
Pacific Film Archive, Berkeley, CA, 1975.
San Francisco Museum of Modern Art,
    San Francisco, 1975.
Vanguard Theater, Los Angeles, 1975.
Pacific Cinematheque, Vancouver, Canada, 1975.
Cineprobe, Museum of Modern Art, NYC, 1975.
Women's Film Festival, Annenberg Center,
    Philadelphia, 1975.
Edinburgh, Berlin, Locarno, Toulon Film
    Festivals, 1975.
Rotterdam Women's Film Festival, Rotterdam,
    Netherlands, 1975.
Arttransition, MIT, Cambridge, MA, 1975.
"In Other Words," Toronto, 1975.
Evenings with Contemporary Filmmakers, AFI,
    JFK Center for the Performing Arts,
    Washington D.C., 1982.
"The Other Avant-Garde," Linz, Austria, 1983.
"Difference: On Representation and Sexuality,"
    Public Theater, NYC, 1985.
National Gallery of Art, Washington D.C., 1988.
"Beyond Illusion: American Independent Film and
    Video Art, 1965 – 75," Whitney Museum of
    American Art, NYC, May 3 – June 3, 1990.
San Francisco Cinematheque, San Francisco,
    (retrospective), 1990.
"Reconsidering the Object of Art: 1965 – 1975"
    Museum of Contemporary Art, Los Angeles,
    1995.
19th Moscow International Film Festival, 1995.
Retrospective, San Francisco Museum of Modern
    Art, San Francisco, April – May, 1997.
Retrospective, Walter Reade Theater, NYC,
    June 20 – 36, 1997.
"Extreme Connoisseurship," Fogg Art Museum,
    Harvard University, Cambridge, MA, 2001.

1976
Kristina Talking Pictures
Cinematographers: Babette Mangolte, Roger Dean

Pacific Film Archive, Berkeley, CA.
Edinburgh Film Festival, Edinburgh, Scotland.
Filmex, Los Angeles.
New American Filmmakers, Whitney Museum
    of American Art, NYC.
Kommunal Kino, Hannover, Germany.
Rotterdam, Berlin, Toronto Film Festivals, 1977.
Museum of Art, Carnegie Institute,
    Pittsburgh, 1977.

1980
Journeys from Berlin/1971
Cinematographer: Carl Teitelbaum

Bleecker Street Cinema, NYC.
Filmworks '80, The Kitchen, NYC.
Art Institute of Chicago.
Rotterdam, Berlin, Edinburgh Film Festivals.
Institute of Contemporary Art, London.
Walker Art Center, Minneapolis, MN.
Collective for Living Cinema, NYC.
Festival of New Cinema, Montreal.
Centre Pompidou, Paris, France.
Boston Film and Video Foundation.
Whitney Museum of American Art Biennial,
    NYC, 1981.
"Aspects of Avant-Garde Film," Academy of
    Motion Picture Arts and Sciences,
    Los Angeles, 1981.
Les Gemeaux Women's Film Festival, Paris, 1981.
"Radical Images," Bleecker Street Cinema,
    NYC, 1981.
"Evenings with Contemporary Filmmakers,"
    AFI, Washington, D.C., 1982.
"Cinema Histories, Cinema Practices," Center
    for 20th Century Studies, University of
    Wisconsin-Milwaukee, WI, 1982.
"A Passage Illuminated: American Avant-Garde
    Film 1980 – 1990," Utrecht, Netherlands,
    1990.
Performance Space, Sydney, 1990
"Shifting the Spectacle: Women, Film, and
    Politics," Carpenter Center for the Visual
    Arts, Harvard University, Cambridge, MA,
    1991.
"Films About Berlin," The Arsenal, Berlin, 1999.
"The Color of Ritual, the Color of Thought:
    Women Avant-Garde Filmmakers in America,
    1930 – 2000," Whitney Museum of
    American Art, NYC, 2000.
"Violence Is at the Margin of All Things,"
    Generali Foundation, Vienna, January – April,
    2002.

1985
The Man Who Envied Women
Cinematographer: Mark Daniels

Montreal Women's Film Festival, Montreal.
Walker Art Center, Minneapolis, MN.
Toronto Film Festival.
Pacific Film Archive. Berkeley, CA.
Roxy Cinema, San Francisco.
Landmark Theater, Buffalo, NY.
Thalia, NYC, 1986.
Agee Room, Bleecker St. Cinema, NYC, 1986.
Berlin and Edinburgh Film Festivals, 1986.
Women's Film Festival, Creteil, France, 1986.
Salsa Majori Film Festival, Italy, 1986.
Political Expression in the Arts, The Johns
    Hopkins University, Baltimore, 1986.
Figueira da Foz Film Festival, Portugal, 1986.
Sheldon Film Theater, Lincoln, NB, 1986.
Nickelodian, Santa Cruz, CA, 1986.
NuArt, Los Angeles, 1986.
Athens, Ohio, Film Festival, 1986.
Cineprobe, Museum of Modern Art, NYC, 1986.
Whitney Museum of American Art, NYC,
    (retrospective), 1986.
Millennium Film Workshop, NYC, 1987.

Whitney Museum of American Art Biennial,
    NYC, 1987.
Sydney Film Festival, 1987.
National Gallery of Art, Washington, D.C., 1988.
"Films in Focus," WNET, 1989.
Performance Space, Sydney,1990.
"The Return of Visual Pleasure," Whitney
    Museum of American Art, NYC, 1991.
Donnell Library, NYC, 1992.
Korea Film Festival, Seoul, Korea, 1994.
Brattle Theater, Cambridge, MA, 1997.
"The Color of Ritual, the Color of Thought:
    Women Avant-Garde Filmmakers in America
    1930 – 2000," Whitney Museum of American
    Art, NYC, July, 2000.

1990
Privilege
Cinematographer: Mark Daniels

Australian Film Institute, Sydney.
State Film Center, Melbourne, Australia.
Union Cinema, Adelaide University, Adelaide,
    Australia.
Australian Film Institute, Perth.
Pacific Film Archive, Berkeley, CA.
Toronto and New York Film Festivals.
Roxy Theater, San Francisco.
Frederick Douglass Institute for African and
    African-American Studies, University of
    Rochester, Rochester, NY.
Virginia Festival of American Film,
    Charlottesville, VA.
Wexner Center for Visual Art, Columbus, OH.
Harvard Film Archive, Carpenter Center for the
    Visual Arts, Cambridge, MA, 1991.
Sundance Film Festival, Park City, UT, 1991.
NuArt, Los Angeles, 1991.
Film Forum, NYC, 1991.
Rotterdam, Berlin, Hong Kong, Locarno Film
    Festivals, 1991.
"Women in the Director's Chair," Chicago
    Filmmakers, Chicago, 1991.
Pacific Rim Consortium on Women's Studies,
    Japan, 1991.
International Documentary Film Festival, Munich,
    1991.
"Shifting the Spectacle: Women, Film, and
    Politics" Carpenter Center for the Visual Arts,
    Harvard University, Cambridge, MA, 1991.
Institute of Contemporary Art, Boston, 1991.
Whitney Museum of American Art Biennial,
    NYC, 1991.
International Festival of Lesbian and Gay Film,
    NYC, 1991.
Montreal Women's Film Festival, 1991.
Yamagata International Documentary Film
    Festival, Japan, 1991.
Institute of Contemporary Art, London, 1991.
Kunstverein, Munich, 1992.
Women's Film Festival, Creteil, France, 1993.
Internacional Films de Dones de Barcelona,
    Barcelona, 1993.
Women Directors with Attitude, Donnell Library,
    NYC, 1993.
Women Make Waves, Taipei, Taiwan, 1993.
Women Directors with Attitude, Donnell Library,
    NYC, 1993.
WNET-TV, 1994.
Taipei Golden Horse Film Festival, Taiwan, 1995.

Film Forum, Los Angeles, 1996.
"Women in Film Colloquium: USA – Vietnam –
    Algeria," Louisiana State University, Baton
    Rouge, 1998.
"The Feminine Eye: Twenty Years of Women's
    Cinema," NY Women in Film and TV,
    Brooklyn Academy of Music, NY, 1999.
"The Time of Our Lives," The New Museum of
    Contemporary Art, NYC, 1999.
"The Color of Ritual, the Color of Thought:
    Women Avant-Garde Filmmakers in America
    1930 – 2000," Whitney Museum of American
    Art, NYC, 2000.

1996
MURDER and murder
Cinematographer: Stephen Kasmierski

Montpelier Dance Festival, Montpelier, France.
Toronto and London Film Festivals.
Chicago Gay and Lesbian Film Festival.
Berlin, Hong Kong, New Zealand Film Festivals,
    1997.
Film Center, Chicago, 1997.
Women's Film Festival, Creteil, France, 1997.
The 4th "Women Make Waves" Film & Video
    Festival, Taipei, Taiwan, 1997.
Boston International Festival of Women's
    Cinema, Brattle Theater, Boston, 1997.
    Inside OUT Lesbian and Gay Film & Video
Festival, Toronto, 1997.
New York, San Francisco, St. Louis, and
    Milwaukee Lesbian and Gay Film Festivals,
    1997.
Women's Film Festival, Minsk, Belarus, 1997.
Northwest Film Forum, Seattle, 1997.
Cinema Zita, Stockholm, Sweden, 1997.
Serralves Museum, Porto, Portugal, 1997.
Paris Lesbian Film Festival, 1997.
Brandeis University, Waltham, MA, 1997.
Anthology Film Archives, NYC, 1997.
Sydney Lesbian and Gay Film Festival, 1998.
"Women in Film Colloquium: USA – Vietnam –
    Algeria," Louisiana State University, Baton
    Rouge, 1998.
Women in the Director's Chair, Walker Art
    Center, Minneapolis, MN, 1998.
Tokyo International Lesbian and Gay Film
    Festival, 1998.
"Feast," Adelaide Lesbian & Gay Cultural
    Festival, Australia, 1998.
Gay and Lesbian Film Festival, Budapest,
    Hungary, 1999.
Cinématheque des Cinéastes, Paris, May, 2002.

2002
After Many a Summer Dies the Swan: Hybrid
(Video Installation, videographers: Charles Atlas,
Natsuko Inue; music: Schoenberg's
"Transfigured Night").

Solo Exhibition: *Yvonne Rainer: Radical
    Juxtapositions 1961 – 2002,*
    Rosenwald–Wolf Gallery, The University
    of the Arts, Philadelphia, October – November.

film retrospectives

1976   Stadtisches Museum, Mönchengladbach,
        Germany

1977   Arsenal, Berlin.

        The Other Cinema, London.

1980   Anthology Film Archive, NYC.

1981   Walker Art Center, Minneapolis, MN.

1982   Institute of Contemporary Art, London.

1985   University of California, Santa Cruz, CA.

1986   Whitney Museum of American Art, NYC.

1988   Boston Museum of Fine Art.

1989   Anthology Film Archive, NYC.

1990   Performance Space, Sydney.
        Australian Film Institute, Melbourne
        and Perth.

        San Francisco Cinematheque, San
        Francisco.

1991   Walker Art Center, Minneapolis, MN.

        Institute of Contemporary Art, London.

        Carnegie Museum of Art, Pittsburgh.

        Cinematheque Ontario, Canada.

1992   Kunstverein, Munich.

1993   Ècole Nationale Supérieure des
        Beaux-arts, Geneva, Switzerland.

1994   Filmcasino, Vienna.
        (sponsored by Synema/ Viennale).

        Kommunalen Kino, Stuttgart, Germany.

1995   American Center, Paris.
        "Traveling Cultures: Sex, Race & the
        Media."

1997   San Francisco Museum of Modern Art,
        San Francisco.

        Film Society of Lincoln Center, Walter
        Reade Theater, NYC.

        Cinema Zita, Stockholm, Sweden.

        Serralves Museum, Porto, Portugal.

        The Brattle Theater, Cambridge, MA.

        University of Maryland Baltimore County.

DanceMagazine
June 1968
75 cents

Awards
Party
Brooklyn
Dance
Boom
Kovach
and
Rabovsky
Today
Views
and
Reviews
of
Young
Choreographers

Yvonne
Rainer
A
Delight
in
Physicality

Dance Magazine,
June 1968
cover photograph:
Zachary Freyman

Afterimage: Drawing Through Process
Notebooks, drawings, videotapes.
Museum of Contemporary Art, Los Angeles,
April 11 – August 22.

*The American Century: Art & Culture
1900 – 2000*
Trio A (video)
Whitney Museum of American Art, NYC,
September 21, 1999 – February 2000.

2000
Afterimage: Drawing Through Process
Notebooks, drawings, videotapes.
Contemporary Arts Museum, Houston,
May 20 – July 23.

2001
A Baroque Party
Inner Appearances (slide and prop installation)
and *Trio A* (video)
Kunsthalle Wien, Vienna, June 11 – September 16.

New York ca. 1975
Projected slides of "Group Hoist" from
Continuous Project – Altered Daily
David Zwirner Gallery, NYC, June 22 – August 3.

Extreme Connoisseurship
Typescript and screening of *Film About a Woman
Who…*
Fogg Art Museum, Harvard University,
Cambridge, MA, December 8 – April 14, 2002.

Show: The Flag
Trio A with Flags (video, 12 performers)
Armory Northwest Gallery, Pasadena, CA,
May 12 – June 16.

group exhibitions –
works other than feature films –
in galleries and museums

1995
Reconsidering the Object of Art 1965 – 75
Trio A (video transfer from 16mm film shot by
Robert Alexander in 1978)
Museum of Contemporary Art, Los Angeles,
October 1995 – January 1996.

1997
Dance Depictions
Trio A (video)
Neuberger Museum of Art, Purchase College,
Purchase, NY, September 7, 1997 – January 11,
1998.

*Minimal Politics: Performativity and Minimalism
in Recent American Art* curated by Maurice
Berger
Dance photos, drawings, videotapes.
Participants: Hans Haacke, Mary Kelly, Robert
Morris, Adrian Piper, Yvonne Rainer.
Fine Arts Gallery, University of Maryland,
Baltimore County, September 25 – January 17.

1999
Mind Moving
Drawings and videotapes.
Participants: Joan Jonas, Babette Mangolte,
Yvonne Rainer.
Galerie Christian Nagel, Koln, Germany,
March 20 – April 18.

solo exhibitions

1998
Yvonne Rainer: Performance into Politics
Dance photos, drawings, videotapes.
Foyer Gallery, Barbican Center, London,
June 10 – July 15.

2001
*24 Photographs of Work by Yvonne Rainer
Taken by Peter Moore*
Bound & Unbound, NYC, June 16 – September 29.

2002
*Yvonne Rainer: Radical Juxtapositions
1961 – 2002*
Video installations, dance photos, drawings,
scores, film clips, and film screenings.
Rosenwald–Wolf Gallery, The University of the
Arts, Philadelphia, October 19 – November 16.

selected bibliography

books by and about Yvonne Rainer

The Films of Yvonne Rainer (scripts by Yvonne Rainer plus essays by Teresa de Laurentis, B. Ruby Rich, and Bérénice Reynaud), Bloomington: Indiana University Press (1989); German translation retitled as: *Talking Pictures: Filme, Feminismus, Psychoanalyse, Avantgarde,* Vienna: Passagen Verlag (1994).

Green, Shelley R.: *Radical Juxtaposition: The Films of Yvonne Rainer,* Metuchen, NJ and London: Scarecrow Press (1994).

Lambert, Carrie: *Yvonne Rainer's Media: Performance and the Image,* Doctoral Dissertation, UMI (Jan. 2002).

Rainer, Yvonne: *Work 1961 – 73,* Halifax: Press of the Nova Scotia College of Art and Design; New York: New York University Press (1974).

Rainer, Yvonne: *A Woman Who... Essays, Interviews, Scripts,* with introductory essays by Judith Mayne and Peggy Phelan, Baltimore: The Johns Hopkins University Press (1999).

articles by Yvonne Rainer

"Yvonne Rainer Interviews Ann Halprin," *Tulane Drama Review* 10:2 (T-30, Winter 1965): 142 – 167; reprinted in *Work 1961 – 73*; and *Happenings and Other Acts,* Mariellen R. Sandford, ed., New York: Routledge (1995).

"Some Retrospective Notes on a Dance for 10 People and 12 Mattresses Called *Parts of Some Sextets*, Performed at the Wadsworth Atheneum, Hartford, Connecticut and Judson Memorial Church, New York, in March 1965," *Tulane Drama Review* 10:2 (T-30, Winter 1965): 168 – 78; reprinted in *Work 1961 – 73*; and *Happenings and Other Acts,* Mariellen R. Sandford, ed., New York: Routledge (1995).

"Notes on Deborah Hay," *Ikon* (Feb. 1967).

"A Quasi Survey of Some 'Minimalist' Tendencies in the Quantitatively Minimal Dance Activity Midst the Plethora, or an Analysis of *Trio A*," *Minimal Art, A Critical Anthology,* Gregory Battcock, ed., New York: E. P. Dutton (1968): 263 – 73; reprinted in *Work 1961 – 73,* 63 – 69; in *Esthetics Contemporary,* Richard Kostelanetz, ed., Buffalo: Prometheus Books (1989): 315 – 19; in *The Twentieth-Century Performance Reader,* Michael Huxley and Noel Witts, eds., New York: Routledge (1996): 290 – 299; in *Minimalism,* James Meyer, ed., New York and London: Phaidon (2000): 235 – 236.

"From an Indian Journal," *Drama Review* 15 (T-50, Spring 1971): 132 – 138; reprinted in *Work 1961 – 73*: 13 – 188.

"Kristina (For a ... Opera)" (photo-romanzo), *Interfunktionen* 12 (1975): 13 – 47.

"Film About a Woman Who..." (script), *October* 2 (Summer 1976): 39 – 67; reprinted in *The Films of Yvonne Rainer* (1989).

"Annotated Selections from the Filmscript of 'Kristina Talking Pictures,'" *No Rose* 1:3 (Spring 1977).

"A Likely Story," *Idiolects* 6 (June 1978).

"Kristina Talking Pictures" (script), *Afterimage* (U.K.) 7 (Summer 1978): 37 – 73; reprinted in *The Films of Yvonne Rainer* (1989).

"Conversation Following Screening at Cinemateque of 'Christina [*sic*] Talking Pictures, April 6, 1978,'" *Cinemanews* 78: 3 – 4 (1978): 16 – 17.

"Paxton Untitled," *Soho Weekly News,* Nov. 16, 1978: 31; reprinted in *Dance Scope* 13 (Winter/Spring 1979): 8 – 10.

"Backwater: Twosome/Paxton and Moss," *Dance Scope* 13 (Winter/Spring 1979).

"Beginning with Some Advertisements for Criticisms of Myself, or Drawing the Dog You May Want to Use to Bite Me With, and Then Going On to Other Matters," *Millennium Film Journal* 6 (Spring 1980): 5 – 7.

"Incomplete Report of the First Week of the Edinburgh International Film Festival, August 17 – 30, 1980 and Musings on Several Other Films," *Idiolects* 9 – 10 (Winter 1980 – 81): 2 – 6.

"Looking Myself in the Mouth," *October* 17 (Summer 1981): 65 – 76.

"More Kicking and Screaming from the Narrative Front/Backwater," *Wide Angle* 7:1 – 2 (Spring 1985): 8 – 12.

"Beyond Mythologies," *Experimental Film Coalition Newsletter* 2:4 (Oct./Nov./Dec. 1985): 3.

"Some Ruminations Around Cinematic Antidotes to the Oedipal Net(tles) while Playing with de Lauraedipus Mulvey, or, He May Be Off-Screen, but...," *Independent* 9:3 (April 1986): 22 – 25; reprinted in *Psychoanalysis and Cinema,* E. Ann Kaplan, ed., New York: Routledge (1990): 188 – 197; and in French translation in *CinemAction* 67: 20 (1993) "Ans de théories féministes sur le cinéma," Bérénice Reynaud and Ginette Vincendeau, eds.: 177 – 182.

"Engineering Calamity with Trisha Brown: An Interview," *Update: Dance/USA* (Oct. 1986): 20 – 22.

"Thoughts on Women's Cinema: Eating Words, Voicing Struggles," *Independent* 10:3 (April 1987): 14 – 16; reprinted in *Blasted Allegories, An Anthology of Writings by Contemporary Artists,* Brian Wallis, ed., New York and Cambridge, MA: New Museum of Contemporary Art and MIT Press (1987): 380 – 385.

"The Man Who Envied Women" (script), *Women and Performance* 3:2 (1988): 103 – 160; reprinted in *The Films of Yvonne Rainer* (1989).

"We Are Demolition Artists: An Interview with Alexander Kluge" (with Ernest Larsen), *Independent (*June 1989): 18 – 25.

"Tea for Two" (with Simone Forti), *Contact Quarterly* 15:2 (Spring/Summer 1990).

"The Work of Art in the (Imagined) Age of Unalienated Exhibition," preface to *Democracy: A Project by Group Material,* Dia Art Foundation, Discussions in Contemporary Culture 5, Seattle: Bay Press (1990).

"Narrative in the (Dis)Service of Identity," *Agenda Contemporary Art Magazine,* Melbourne (May 1991): 12 – 14.

"Working Round the L-Word," *Queer Looks: Perspectives on Lesbian and Gay Film and Video,* Martha Gever, John Greyson, and Pratibha Parmar, eds., New York: Routledge (1993): 12 – 20.

"Privilege" (filmscript), *Screen Writings: Scripts and Texts by Independent Filmmakers,* Scott MacDonald, ed., Berkeley: University of California Press (1995): 273 – 332.

"The Avant-Garde Humpty Dumpty," http://www.thecity.sfsu.edu/users/XFactor/ participants/participants.html (1996).

"MURDER and murder" (script), *Performing Arts Journal* 55 (1997): 76 – 117.

"Skirting," *The Feminist Memoir Project: Voices from Women's Liberation,* New York: Crown Press (1998).

"Pedagogical Vaudeville #3," *PAJ, a Journal of Performance and Art* 23: 67/1 (Jan. 2001): 48 – 61.

"Two Bodies," *Magnetic North: Canadian Experimental Video* (catalogue, Walker Art Center), Jenny Lion, ed., Minneapolis: University of Minnesota Press (2001): 126 – 127.

"A Fond Memoir with Sundry Reflections on a Friend and Her Art," *Trisha Brown: Dance and Art in Dialogue, 1965 – 2000,* Addison Gallery of American Art and MIT Press (Fall 2002).

other writings by Yvonne Rainer

Letter to *Artforum* 12:16 (Sept. 1973): 10.

"Response to Coco Fusco's 'Fantasies of Oppositionality,'" *Screen* 30:3 (Summer 1989): 91 – 98.

Letter to Shu Lea Cheang and Kathy High, *Felix* 1:2 (Spring 1992): 27 – 29.

Letter to *October* 71 "Feminist Issues" (Winter 1995).

interviews with Yvonne Rainer

Austin, Linda and Anya Pryor: "Token Minimalist Dancing Girl: Yvonne Rainer talks with…" *Movement Research Performance Journal* 16 (Spring 1998): 15.

Bear, Liza and Willoughby Sharp: "The Performer as a Persona: An Interview with Yvonne Rainer," *Avalanche* 5 (Summer 1972): 46 – 59.

Blumenthal, Lyn: "On Art and Artists: Yvonne Rainer," *Profile* 4:5 (1984).

Briggs, Kate and Fiona MacDonald: "Three Possible Endings: An Interview with Yvonne Rainer," *Photofile* (Australia) 30 (Winter 1990): 28 – 33.

Buchman, Sabeth: "Das Pendel Steht Nicht Still: Ein Interview mit Yvonne Rainer," *Texte Zur Kunst* 39 (Sept. 2000).

Camera Obscura Collective: "Yvonne Rainer: Interview," *Camera Obscura* 1 (Fall 1976): 76 – 96.

Carroll, Noël: "Interview with a Woman Who…" *Millennium Film Journal* 7/8/9 (Fall 1980 – Winter 1981): 37 – 68; reprinted in *A Woman Who: Essays, Interviews, Scripts* (1999).

Easterwood, Kurt, Susanne Fairfax, and Laura Poitras: "Yvonne Rainer: Declaring Stakes," *San Francisco Cinematheque (*1990).

Goodeve, Thyrza Nichols: "Rainer Talking Pictures," *Art in America* 85:7 (July 1997): 56 – 63, 104.

Griffin, Tim: "Interview with Y. R.," *Index* 5 (April 2002): 94 – 101.

Jayamanne, Laleen, with Geeta Kapur and Yvonne Rainer: "Discussing Modernity, 'Third World,' and 'The Man Who Envied Women,'" *Art and Text* 23:4 (March – May 1987): 41 – 51.

Laderman, David: "Interview with Yvonne Rainer," *Art Papers* 13:3 (May/June 1989): 18 – 24.

_____: "Contents Under Pressure: A Conversation with Yvonne Rainer," *Documents* 18 (Fall 1999): 6 – 16.

MacDonald, Scott: "Yvonne Rainer (interview on Privilege)," *Critical Cinema* 2, Berkeley: University of California Press (1992): 344 – 354.

Mekas, Jonas: "Interview with Yvonne Rainer," *Village Voice* (April 25, 1974): 77.

Mitchell, Robb: "Representing Women: An Interview with Yvonne Rainer," *Screenline* (Winter 1990/1991).

Pontbriand, Chantal: "Interview with Yvonne Rainer," *Parachute* 10 (Spring 1978).

Rosenbaum, Mitchell: "Interview with Yvonne Rainer." *Persistence of Vision* 6 (Summer 1988); reprinted in *The Films of Yvonne Rainer* (1989).

Sanchez, George Emilio: "Aborting Elevation: A Talk with Yvonne Rainer," *Movement Research Performance Journal* 20 (Winter/Spring 2000): 8.

Soffer, Shirley: "'You Gave Me So Much Room': A Reminiscence with Yvonne Rainer," *Helicon Nine* 20 (Summer 1989): 92 – 107.

Tillman, Lynne: "A Woman Called Yvonne," *Village Voice* (Jan. 15, 1991).

Walworth, Dan: "A Conversation with Yvonne Rainer," *Psychcritique* 2:1 (1987): 1 – 16.